THE
SKY-RELIGION IN
EGYPT

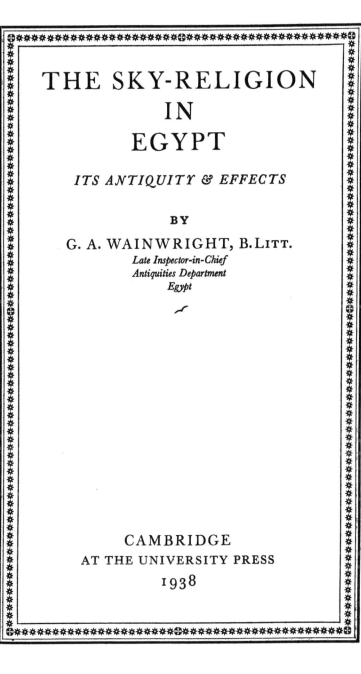

THE SKY-RELIGION
IN
EGYPT

ITS ANTIQUITY & EFFECTS

BY

G. A. WAINWRIGHT, B.Litt.

Late Inspector-in-Chief
Antiquities Department
Egypt

CAMBRIDGE
AT THE UNIVERSITY PRESS
1938

CAMBRIDGE UNIVERSITY PRESS
Cambridge, New York, Melbourne, Madrid, Cape Town,
Singapore, São Paulo, Delhi, Tokyo, Mexico City

Cambridge University Press
The Edinburgh Building, Cambridge CB2 8RU, UK

Published in the United States of America by Cambridge University Press, New York

www.cambridge.org
Information on this title: www.cambridge.org/9780521237512

© Cambridge University Press 1938

First published 1938
First paperback edition 2011

A catalogue record for this publication is available from the British Library

ISBN 978-0-521-23751-2 Paperback

CONTENTS

ILLUSTRATIONS

PLATES

PREFACE

THE present work has grown out of a long series of articles published in the *Journal of Egyptian Archaeology* and elsewhere from 1928 to 1935. The writing of these happened to coincide largely with the preparation of Dr Margaret A. Murray's book *The God of the Witches*. Many discussions with her of the bearing of many details opened up for me long vistas of possibilities in my own line of research. The result was that I began to see that suggestions of what she calls the Old Religion were to be extricated here and there from such records as we have of ancient Egyptian religion and history. At present it is not much that has come to light, and that little has been complicated hitherto by attempts to interpret much of it as Osiris-worship. This it was not, except in so far as scraps were assimilated here and there. As we get used to the idea more may appear. The fewness of the scraps is probably accounted for by the fact that the religion here revealed was extremely ancient and, as in recent Europe, it had ceased to be that of the ruling classes, but continued as that of the masses, and of neighbouring lands. The masses were unlettered, and Egypt's neighbours, Libya and Ethiopia, were not only unlettered but barbarous as well. Hence, it is not surprising that their thoughts and manners and customs have not found utterance in the writings of the learned, or in those of the two dominant religions, Rê- and Osiris-worship. Under the conditions it is perhaps surprising that so much should have come to expression in one way or another. The information is preserved mostly as scraps, survivals from a previous period, largely as odds and ends which have been annexed by the dominant religions. The great source of information proves to be the writings of the classical authors, whose records consist mostly of folk-memory and of practices which interested the populace. In these writings we get a view of Egypt other than that usually presented by the official inscriptions.

It is hoped that the following pages will appeal both to the Egyptologist and to a larger world. This entails certain difficulties, for much that is commonplace to the Egyptologist is unknown to the outside world, and conversely what is self-evident, let us say, to the ethnologist is completely unthought of by the majority of Egyptologists. The indulgence of each must, therefore, be craved for the labouring of details which must appear to them as tiresome and unnecessary. Similarly, though one would prefer the correct reproduction of various Egyptian words, they have been anglicized both for the sake of the non-Egyptologist and for simplicity in printing.

The Greek forms of names have been kept for the legendary figures of the classical tales, while some form of the Egyptian name has been used for the historic kings. Thus, the reader will find both Khufu and Cheops, Menkaurê and Mycerinus, Neithaqert and Nitocris, Shabaka and Sabacon. Sesostris is a purely legendary character, whose name seems to have been derived from that of the Senusrets of the Twelfth Dynasty, but whose exploits have been founded on those of Ramesses II. The same method has been followed with regard to the gods. Amûn and Ammon are the same personages, as are Seth and Typhon, Wazet and Buto. The one form of name refers to the deity as known to Egyptology, the other to that deity as seen through the Greek writings.

A conspectus of the periods, dynasties, and dates is

appended, and the reader is begged to bear in mind the *caveat* which introduces it.

I have already acknowledged my debt to Dr Murray for giving me a new outlook on the possibilities. This assistance was indirect, and I now have the pleasant duty of acknowledging the direct help given me by Mr R. O. Faulkner and Mr W. F. J. Knight. Both Mr Faulkner with the hieroglyphs and Mr Knight with the classical texts have never stinted the help of their profound knowledge, whenever I have submitted difficulties to them. The uncertainties are of course greater in the hieroglyphic texts, especially in such passages as those which I believe to deal with my subject-matter. The passages themselves are few, the language of the Pyramid Texts is archaic, and deals with a subject of which we have hitherto had no inkling. Moreover, the knowledge of the language is as yet nothing like so precise as is that of Greek and Latin. I trust there are no mistakes in the renderings here put forward or in the deductions made from them, but, if there are, they will be mine not theirs.

G. A. WAINWRIGHT

LONDON
October 1937

CONSPECTUS OF DATES

For the convenience of those unfamiliar with Egyptian history a conspectus is added of the periods, dynasties, and kings mentioned in the text. Dates are given, but it must not be imagined that they are exact. In fact the further we go back beyond the Twelfth Dynasty the wider become the various estimates, for estimates are all that those dates are. After the rise of the Eighteenth Dynasty the dates are probably accurate within a few years. With these provisos the following dates are submitted which gain a good deal of credence, and are certainly sufficiently accurate for the present purposes.

MERIMDIAN, FAYYUMI, BADARIAN AGES   beginning say 5000 B.C.

FIRST PREDYNASTIC AGE (Amratian, Naqadah I)

SECOND PREDYNASTIC AGE (Gerzean, Naqadah II)

ARCHAIC PERIOD AND RISE OF THE DYNASTIES
    Scorpion King

    FIRST DYNASTY   say 3400 B.C.
       Narmer
       Udymu (Den)

    SECOND DYNASTY
       Nebrê
       Neterymu (Neteren)
       Perabsen
       Karê
       Khasekhem = Khasekhemui

    THIRD DYNASTY   say 2980–2900 B.C.
       Nebkarê
       Zoser
       Sneferu

CONSPECTUS OF DATES

OLD KINGDOM

FOURTH DYNASTY	say 2900–2750 B.C.
Khufu (Cheops)	
Dadfrê	
Khafrê (Chephren)	
Menkaurê (Mycerinus)	
Shepseskaf	
FIFTH DYNASTY	say 2750–2625 B.C.
Userkaf	
Sahurê	
Neferirkarê	
Neuserrê	
Dadkarê	
SIXTH DYNASTY	say 2625–2475 B.C.
Pepi	
Neithaqert (Nitocris)	

MIDDLE KINGDOM

ELEVENTH DYNASTY	say 2160–2000 B.C.
Mentuhotep I	

HYKSOS PERIOD	say 1788–1580 B.C.

NEW KINGDOM

EIGHTEENTH DYNASTY

Tethmosy III	1501–1447 B.C.
Tethmosy IV	1420–1411 B.C.
Amenhotep III	1411–1375 B.C.
Akhenaton (Amenhotep IV)	1375–1369 B.C.
Tutankhaton = Tutankhamûn	1369–1360 B.C.

NINETEENTH DYNASTY

Ramesses II	1292–1225 B.C.
Merenptah	1225–1215 B.C.

TWENTIETH DYNASTY

Ramesses III	1198–1167 B.C.

TWENTY-FIRST DYNASTY

Herihor	1090–1085 B.C.

LIBYAN PERIOD, ETHIOPIAN PERIOD, ETC.

TWENTY-SECOND DYNASTY

Sheshonk I	945–924 B.C.

[xiv]

CONSPECTUS OF DATES

LIBYAN ANCESTOR settling in Ethiopia	*c.* 920 B.C.
PIANKHI in Ethiopia	*c.* 744–710 B.C.
TWENTY-THIRD DYNASTY	
Osorkon III	*c.* 720 B.C.
TWENTY-FOURTH DYNASTY	
Bocchoris (Bekenrenef, Wahkarê)	718–712 B.C.
TWENTY-FIFTH DYNASTY	
Shabaka (Sabacon)	712–700 B.C.
TWENTY-SIXTH DYNASTY	
Amasis	569–525 B.C.
ERGAMENES in Ethiopia	*c.* 240–215 B.C.

ABBREVIATIONS

Anns. Serv.   *Annales du Service des Antiquités de l'Égypte*, le Caire.

Aucher.   J. B. Aucher, *Eusebii Pamphili Caesariensis Episcopi Chronicon Bipartitum*, Venice, 1818.

B. *A.R.*   Breasted, *Ancient Records of Egypt*, Chicago, 1906.

Bissing and Kees, *Re-Heiligtum*.   von Bissing und Kees, *Das Re-Heiligtum des Königs Ne-woser-re (Rathures)*, Bände II, III, Leipzig, 1923, 1928.

Dindorf.   Dindorf, *Georgius Syncellus* in *Corpus Scriptorum Historiae Byzantinae*, Pars VII, 1, Bonn, 1829.

Frazer, *The Magic Art*; *Taboo*; *The Dying God*; *Adonis, Attis, Osiris*; *Spirits of the Corn and of the Wild*; *Balder the Beautiful*. Refer to the Third edition of *The Golden Bough*.

Griffith, *Studies*.   *Studies Presented to F. Ll. Griffith*, London, 1932.

JEA.   *The Journal of Egyptian Archaeology*, London.

JRAI.   *The Journal of the Royal Anthropological Institute of Great Britain and Ireland*, London.

L. *D*.   C. R. Lepsius, *Denkmäler aus Aegypten und Aethiopien*, Berlin, 1849-58.

OLZ.   *Orientalistische Literaturzeitung*, Leipzig.

Pyr., Pyramid Texts.   Sethe, *Die altaegyptischen Pyramidentexte*, Leipzig, 1910.

Rec. de Trav.   *Recueil de travaux relatifs à la philologie et à l'archéologie égyptiennes et assyriennes*, Paris.

Roscher, *Lexikon*.   W. H. Roscher, *Ausführliches Lexikon der griechischen und römischen Mythologie*, Leipzig.

Schoene.   A. Schoene, *Eusebi Chronicorum Libri Duo*, Berlin, 1875.

Wilkinson, *M. and C.*   Sir J. G. Wilkinson, *The Manners and Customs of the Ancient Egyptians*, vol. III, London, 1878.

ZÄS.   *Zeitschrift für ägyptische Sprache und Altertumskunde*, Leipzig.

ZDMG.   *Zeitschrift der deutschen Morgenländischen Gesellschaft*, Leipzig.

GENERALITIES

HERE in the north in our chilly, wet, climate we are accustomed to think of the sun as the natural object of worship as being the obvious giver of life. So natural an idea is encouraged by a knowledge of the sun-worship which was so marked a development in the later phases of classical heathendom.[1] Such, however, is not the view taken by dwellers in Africa. In these hot lands the sun is the enemy of mankind, scorching up everything. In antiquity certain Libyans, the Atarantes, cursed the sun (Hdt. IV, 184), as did some of the Ethiopians of Meroë (Diod. III, 9; Strabo, XVII, ii, § 3). Similarly, among the modern Bari of the White Nile unduly prolonged sunshine is thought to be the work of a malevolent rainmaker. One, a certain Yokwe Kerri, was accused of 'willing sun' and so counteracting the efforts of a benevolent practitioner,[2] and the people sought out another, Lako by name, to take vengeance on him for the same offence. To his superior's efforts to save him they replied: 'It is nothing to do with God: it is Lako who is shining.'[3] What is earnestly desired in these countries, and what these rainmakers were considered to be withholding, is the rain. It is that which gives life to the parched ground, to the crops, the animals, and men. Hence it is that the rain itself, or the Sky which sends

---

[1] By the end nearly every god had been so solarized that it is no easy matter to disentangle his original nature. In Egypt also religious history during Pharaonic times is largely one of encroachment by the sun on the Old Religion, which latter consisted in the worship of the sky and its phenomena, and of fertility.

[2] Seligman, *Pagan Tribes of the Nilotic Sudan*, p. 295.

[3] Id. *op. cit.* p. 289.

it, is the Giver of Life, and in due time develops into a god. Thus, one of the two highest spiritual agencies of the Dinka on the White Nile is called *Dengdit* or merely *Deng*, words which literally mean 'Great Rain';[1] by one of the Nuba tribes the creator god is called *Kalo*, which similarly means 'Rain';[2] the Suk call their supreme god and creator *Torôrut*, 'the Sky', who is also called *Ilat*, 'Rain';[3] and the Gallas call theirs *Wâq*, a word which originally means 'Heaven'.[4] In the same way the Nuer use an expression for 'it will rain' which is literally 'God falls',[5] as do the Beir of the Sobat River.[6] Higher even than *Deng*, who is however intimately related to him, is *Nhialic*, the creator and organizer of the world. Literally translated his name merely means 'in the above', and he lives in the 'Rain-place', whence he sends the rain.[7] In fact all over East Africa the sky-god who sends the rain is supreme, and apart from ancestor-worship, religion is a question of rainmaking. Except for one small enclave on the Abyssinian frontier, Professor Seligman has been unable to discover any signs of sun-worship in the Sudan.[8] This concern with the sky and its doings is so primitive that there is hardly a corner of the earth whither man has not carried it. In Egypt, as will be seen, it goes back to the earliest times for which we can deduce any religion at all.

Actually the sky-religion is part and parcel of man's preoccupation with his own health and wealth. On the

[1] Seligman, *Pagan Tribes*, p. 179.   [2] Id. *op. cit.* p. 394.
[3] M. W. H. Beech, *The Suk*, p. 19, though others say that Ilat is the son or servant of Torôrut, while yet others only know of Ilat.
[4] Littmann in Hastings, *Encyclopaedia of Religion and Ethics*, s.v. *Abyssinia*, p. 56. von Tiling has a useful study of him in *OLZ*, 1926, cols. 947–9.
[5] Seligman, *Pagan Tribes*, p. 234.
[6] Id. *op. cit.* p. 361.   [7] Id. *op. cit.* p. 179.
[8] Seligman, *Egypt and Negro Africa*, p. 12.

proper functioning of the weather depends the propitiousness of the seasons, hence the fertility of the soil, which gives increase to the game and wild fruits for the hunters, and to the herds and crops for the pastoralists and agriculturists. This enables man in his turn to 'be fruitful, and multiply, and replenish the earth, and subdue it', and entails the tribe's general welfare, whether expressed in the absence of epidemics or in success in war. In later times this twofold character, as we are liable to think it, of sky and fertility is still clear in the nature of many deities. Thus, in Egypt Seth, the storm-god, was concerned with tilling the earth, as will be seen on pp. 27, 29, 30, and Min was both sky- and fertility-god. Sandan fulfilled both functions in Cilicia, as did Zeus Adados at Baalbek in Syria.[1] Zeus himself, the personified sky, had a sacred oak at his famous shrine of Dodona. In modern Siam the Mock King's title is 'Lord of the Heavenly Hosts', and it is he who ploughs the nine furrows and whose behaviour controls the weather for the coming year.[2] He is thus very like Seth. In Europe the 'witches' of the ancient pre-Christian religion are best remembered today for their fertility-rites and concern with animals, but they also professed to have power over the elements, to be able to raise storms, etc., etc.[3]

At a very lowly stage in his progress man undertakes to control the phenomena of the sky on which so much

[1] Wainwright in *JEA*, XXI, pp. 152–4, where other cases are quoted.
[2] Frazer, *The Dying God*, pp. 149, 155, 156.
[3] M. A. Murray, *The Witch-cult in Western Europe*, Index, s.v. *Rainmaking, Storm-raising*; id. *The God of the Witches*, pp. 149 ff.; Frazer, *The Magic Art*, I, pp. 322, 326, 329; J. Grimm, *Teutonic Mythology* (trans. Stallybrass), pp. 1086–8. Perhaps the best-known reference to this belief is by Macbeth (Act IV, Scene I), who conjures the witches thus: 'Though you untie the winds, and let them fight against the churches; etc., etc.'

[3]

depends; the beneficent warmth, rain, and pleasant breezes, and the dangerous thunder, lightning, hail, tempest, and excessive or untimely cold. The wielder of this power is also expected to keep his people free of epidemics.[1] This power of control is vested in a certain individual, who in virtue of this power develops from a rainmaker into a priest-king. This office in its turn breaks up into its component parts of priest on the one hand and king on the other.

The possession of this power makes the priest-king divine. Then, as religious ideas develop and anthropomorphic gods in heaven emerge, the priest or king becomes the god incarnate here on earth, where he acts for his heavenly prototype. But here a difficulty supervenes, for man, even the most divine, is but mortal. Hence, the divinity within him would grow old and feeble as its human shrine became more decrepit and infirm. As this cannot be allowed, the holder should lay down his life whilst still in his prime, so as to pass on the power to his successor in its full vigour. This he often has to do even today, but throughout the world and down the ages the details of the divine death have come to suffer many modifications. This has been brought about by such things as the progress of religious thought, the interweaving of the doctrines of other religious systems, and finally by the ability of the victim to escape his fate. At last it comes to be realized that, the powers within him being magical, they can be renewed by magic, or can be transferred to a substitute who lays down his life for him. Such a man may offer himself willingly; be recognized by certain well-known marks; belong to a family devoted to, and

---

[1] Seligman, *Egypt and Negro Africa*, pp. 6, 47. The Nuer call the cattle plague *diu*, which is almost certainly the name of a sky-spirit, id. *Pagan Tribes*, p. 232. The rainmaking ceremony ensures fertility to the Bari and banishes disease and want, id. *op. cit.* p. 281.

honoured for, this service; be a criminal, who, already having been condemned to death, would have to die in any case. Very often strangers are made to undertake the penalty, for which purpose captives taken in war are peculiarly suitable. Animal sacrifices take the place of human ones. Finally, it is realized that it is not the man himself who matters, but his office. At this stage it is only his insignia which is sacrificed and the wearer escapes, or it may be that the sacrifice is carried out on an effigy. In fact by this time the ceremony has often almost lost all magical or religious significance, and has degenerated into nothing but a popular festival. The human substitute is generally given a period during which he is treated as royalty and enjoys a mock kingship.[1]

The manner and period of the divine death vary greatly. Very often the king has to commit suicide at the appointed time; as among the Banyankole and Bakitara of Uganda, the Balobedu of South Africa, or the king of Sofala also in South Africa.[2] Sometimes he is slain by his successor; as among the Fung of the Blue Nile,[3] the Shilluks of the White Nile,[4] the Banyankole of Uganda at one time,[5] or as the divine priest 'The King of the Wood' at Nemi in ancient Italy.[6] Among the first three peoples the successor must be of the blood royal, but at Nemi in classical times he had to be a runaway slave. Only too often the divine victim is burned to death. This happened all over heathen Europe under the ancient fertility- and sky-religion known to us as

[1] See pp. 58 ff. *infra* for all this in detail.
[2] Seligman, *Egypt and Negro Africa*, pp. 30, 32, 34, 35.
[3] Id. *Pagan Tribes*, pp. 426–8.
[4] Id. *op. cit.* p. 90. The son of the rainmaker of the Malwal Dinka seems to take a prominent part in his father's death, id. *Egypt and Negro Africa*, p. 23.
[5] Id. *op. cit.* p. 34.   [6] Frazer, *The Magic Art*, I, p. 11.

the 'witch' cult.[1] The divine king of the ancient Prussians used to burn himself to death, lighting the fire with his own hand.[2] Hercules was a storm-god,[3] and he burned himself to death on a pyre on the top of Mount Oeta in Thessaly. The conflagration was increased by the thunderbolts which fell from the atmosphere, and he ascended to heaven in a cloud while the thunder rolled.[4] In Cilicia Sandan, the

sky- and fertility-god of the *labrys* ⋈ was periodically

burned on the pyre.[5] Melcarth was burned in effigy at Tyre, where he was also represented by Hercules,[6] and in whose temple was the stela of *smaragdus* suitable to a sky-god.[7] In Egypt it will be seen that Seth, the storm-god, had been liable to death, and tradition states that that death had been by fire (p. 53). But in historic times he, and the Pharaoh his representative, were able to escape.

---

[1] M. A. Murray, *Witch-cult*, pp. 159–62; id. *The God of the Witches*, pp. 135, 136.

[2] Frazer, *The Dying God*, pp. 41, 42.

[3] The chief god of Meroë we know to have been Amûn, but Strabo, XVII, 2, § 3, calls him Hercules. Diodorus, III, 9, includes both Hercules and Zeus among the chief gods there. Hercules also seems to have been identified with Shu, Roeder in Roscher, *Lexikon*, s.v. *Schow*, col. 571; Kees in Pauly-Wissowa, *Real-Encyclopädie*, s.v. *Sos*, col. 1143. He cannot be separated from the thunder-gods Indra and Thor, von Schroeder in *Denkschr. K. Ak. Wiss. in Wien, Phil-hist. Klasse*, 1914, Band 58, Abhandl. 3, pp. 106, 109. The *labrys* of Zeus Labrayndeus himself had passed through Hercules' hands, Plutarch, *Quaest. Graeci*, 45.

[4] Diodorus Siculus, IV, 38, 4; Apollodorus, *Bibliotheca*, II, 7, 7. In his edition of Apollodorus (I, pp. 270, 271, notes 1, 2) Frazer discusses the literature in great detail. The site of the pyre has been found, see p. 64, note 1, *infra*.

[5] Frazer, *Adonis, Attis, Osiris*, I, p. 126.

[6] Id. *op. cit.* I, p. 111.

[7] Herodotus, II, 44; Wainwright in *JEA*, xx, p. 147; id. in *Palestine Exploration Fund: Quarterly Statement*, 1934, pp. 42, 43.

All the world over the central practice of the sky- and fertility-religion is the sacrifice of the divine king, either in his own person or in that of a substitute. Very little research, however, has been done on this great system in Egypt. Indeed, until quite recently this whole background and substratum of Egyptian religion had been ignored. Detailed study had been confined in the first place to the well-known Osiris-religion, which overrode almost everything else as time went on, and in the second place to the sun-worship, which became so prominent as the royal religion. The multitude of other gods have been relegated to a vague limbo, and have been seen incomprehensibly as they appeared in the light of these other systems. Moret has broached the subject of the sacrifice of the god in many of his studies,[1] but he thinks of it in terms of the Osiris-religion. My own work has shown that the sky- and fertility-religion of Egypt included some of her most ancient gods. The intention of this enquiry is to examine some scraps of evidence that it is aboriginal in that country, being in fact even more ancient than Egypt herself, and that the divine victim had been sacrificed there as elsewhere.

[1] E.g. *Kings and Gods of Egypt, Mystères égyptiens, From Tribe to Empire, La mise à mort du dieu en Égypte.*

THE
SKY-RELIGION IN EGYPT

IN the beginning Egypt was not. In those days the Nile Valley was an uninhabitable swamp, full of waterfowl and infested by the hippopotamus, crocodile, and such a marsh-dweller as the wild pig. In palaeolithic days large parts of the vast Sahara had been steppe or parkland eminently suitable for the existence of game, and also of primitive man, who has left signs of his presence everywhere. The palaeolithic, and indeed the neolithic, people inhabited what is now the desert.[1] This state of affairs lasted late, even into the settled times of the Fayyumi and Merimdian cultures, which flourished and grew corn in what is now the high desert.[2] In those days the inundation of the Nile, if there were one, did not affect the crops, for they were growing on the high land far above its reach. They were dependent for their growth upon the rains of heaven, and these were abundant, for in those days North Africa was in the pluvial zone much as Europe is today.

The beginnings of 'Egypt' are, therefore, outside the Nile Valley, and as life in the Sahara became progressively more difficult, so man began to turn to the 'desert' edges of the Nile swamp. At this edge we find settlements of those

[1] Moret gives a general sketch of these conditions in Moret and Davy, *From Tribe to Empire*, pp. 115–22. For more detail see Caton-Thompson and Gardner in *The Geographical Journal*, LXXX, pp. 369–406; K. S. Sandford, *Palaeolithic Man and the Nile Valley in Upper and Middle Egypt*, pp. 95, 96, 105, 106.

[2] Caton-Thompson and Gardner, *The Desert Fayum, passim*, especially pp. 89–93; Junker, e.g. in *Vorläufiger Bericht über...Merimde-Benisalâme (Ak. der Wiss. in Wien, Phil.-hist. Klasse, Anzeiger, 1930)*, pp. 40, 41 and Pl. III.

peoples we now call Badarians, First Predynastic (Amratian), and Second Predynastic (Gerzean). Thus the closeness of the relations between Libya and Egypt, which is well known throughout Pharaonic days, was even more intimate before the dawn of history. In fact Libya was the 'Egypt' of those days.

My studies of the Egyptian sky-religion have shown it to have been extremely ancient. In fact, many of the gods encountered are so ancient that they were lost during historic times, or at best had become such shadowy figures that they appear to us as little more than names. Junker has recently shown that there had been a nameless sky-god who was already fusing in Protodynastic times with the hawk-god to form a compound deity, Horus. He was merely called ⸗, 'The Great (or Greatest) God',[1] and so represents a gradual personification of the primitive vague idea of the Power of the Sky. Much has been seen of the Bull of the Sky, and bulls were clearly already sacred in Badarian times[2] and at Merimdah.[3] The Double-axe, which elsewhere as the *labrys* became the symbol of the thunder-god, was already sacred in prehistoric Egypt, though it had died out by the end of the Old Kingdom.[4] There were also the

---

[1] Junker, *Giza*, II, p. 48.

[2] Wainwright in *JEA*, XIX, 42–52; XXI, 158–65. Bulls were among the animals carefully wrapped up and buried in Badarian days, Brunton and Caton-Thompson, *The Badarian Civilisation and Predynastic Remains near Badari*, p. 42. Cf. also pp. 91 ff., where Miss Caton-Thompson records many burials of young cattle in Old Kingdom times.

[3] Junker in *Ak. der Wiss. in Wien, Phil.-hist. Klasse, Anzeiger*, 1933, p. 81.

[4] Wainwright in *JEA*, XVII, p. 192. The axe, single at any rate, was sacred to the extent of providing an amulet already in Fayyumi A times, Caton-Thompson and Gardner, *The Desert Fayum*, Pl. xxxiii, 12 and pp. 82, 20. Cf. also Pls. xxxiii, 11, xxxiv, 1, 2, 3, pp. 20, 77, 83, though there is no attempt at boring these for suspension. Today the

Mountains, from which no doubt the Pharaonic mountain-god, Ḥꜣ, developed,[1] and Ꜣš or šꜣ, a mysterious form or relative of Seth.[2] Another was Mḫnty-n-írty at the Thunder-bolt-city of Letopolis, who in Pyramid times was being replaced by Horus, and whose name is mostly known to us as an epithet of Horus. Horus the Elder is not much better, and almost all we know of the Sky-pole, wḫ, is that it had preceded Hathor at Cusae, where she had been the goddess from the Twelfth Dynasty onwards.[3]

But two of these sky-gods lasted on in full vigour down to the end of Pharaonic history. These are Seth and Min, and they or their prototypes take us back to the earliest age at which we are able to see any details of the primitive inhabitants' way of life. Thus, the pig and the hippopota-mus were both sacred to the storm-god Seth. All through Pharaonic times the pig was rare and an abomination, but at Merimdah and Maadi he was common and a food animal.[4] The pig was also painted on the C pottery of the First Predynastic civilization,[5] at which time the mys-

single axe still acts as a rainstone in some parts of the Sudan, Seligman, *Pagan Tribes*, pp. 467, 476, 477, 480. Three such axes, of haematite, from the Azande were sent by General Gordon with the statement that they were 'stones fallen from the sky' and were cult objects. They are now in the Cairo Museum, Daressy in *Anns. Serv.* XXII, pp. 157 ff.

[1] Wainwright in *JEA*, XXI, pp. 161, 162.

[2] Newberry in *JEA*, XIV, pp. 220, 221 and figs. 7–12; Shorter in *JEA*, XI, p. 78; Murray in *Ancient Egypt and the Near East*, 1934, pp. 115–17.

[3] Wainwright in *JEA*, XXI, p. 168; Blackman, *Meir*, I, p. 2.

[4] Menghin and Amer, *Excavations of the Egyptian University in the Neolithic Site at Maadi*, p. 52 (Egyptian University, Faculty of Arts, Publication No. 19).

[5] Scharff in *ZÄS*, LXI, pp. 17, 18 and fig. 1, where they are called donkeys on the strength of the bristles on the back. But the pig had bristles, which Pharaonic art shows clearly, cf. Spiegelberg and Newberry, *Excavations in the Theban Necropolis*, Pl. xiii; Newberry in *JEA*, XIV, Pl. xviii, 3, and cf. Pl. xix several times. While the general

terious Seth-animal itself was already figured at least twice.[1] Seth's other animal, the hippopotamus, was one of the commonest subjects treated by the artist of the First Pre-dynastic Age,[2] and a Badarian amulet may be intended to represent him.[3] He was one of the food animals of both the Fayyumis and Merimdians.[4] Further, at Maadi and on several occasions at Merimdah-Beni-Salamah hippopotamus leg-bones have been found set upright. It is, therefore, evident that already in those early days the animal was either sacred, as Menghin supposes,[5] or at least that it was acceptable to the god, as Junker supposes.[6] Hence, the originals of the historic storm-god, Seth, were already prominent when we get our earliest glimpse of life on the 'desert' bordering the Nile swamp.

The sky- and fertility-god, Min, was very similar, for he was fully developed by Archaic days, c. 3500 B.C., while the

appearance is admittedly more asinine than porcine, the upright tail is characteristic of the boar, id. op. cit. p. 218, but scarcely of the donkey. The donkey does not appear to be early in Egypt, for it was not found at Merimdah which is Fayyumi A Culture (5000–4500 B.C.). It was found, however, in Late Predynastic times at Maadi, Menghin, *Merimde-Beni-Salame and Maadi* in *Ak. der Wiss. in Wien, Phil.-hist. Klasse, Anzeiger*, 1933, p. 88. The earliest assimilation of the Seth-animal to the donkey yet known is in the early Middle Kingdom, Newberry, *op. cit.* p. 224, fig. 17 and note 1. But whether pig or donkey, it is clearly the Seth-animal, which is what concerns us here.

[1] Ayrton and Loat, *The Predynastic Cemetery at el Mahasna*, Pl. xii, 2 and p. 27; Scharff in *ZÄS*, LXI, p. 17, fig. 1, and p. 23.

[2] Petrie, *Prehistoric Egypt*, p. 12. Cf. p. 16, where more hippopotami are listed than any other animal.

[3] Brunton and Caton-Thompson, *The Badarian Civilisation*, p. 27 and Pl. xxiv, 15.

[4] Caton-Thompson, *The Desert Fayum*, p. 34; Junker in *Ak. der Wiss. in Wien, Phil.-hist. Klasse, Anzeiger*, 1929, p. 218.

[5] *Mitt. des deutschen Inst. für Äg. Altertumskunde in Kairo*, III, p. 151.

[6] *Ak. der Wiss. in Wien, Phil.-hist. Klasse, Anzeiger*, 1933, pp. 80, 81. Cf. *Anzeiger*, 1934, p. 132.

double or multiple arrow which developed into his thunder-bolt was already sacred by the middle of the Second Predynastic (Gerzean) period.[1] The corn, which was his special care, was not the good wheat $sw \cdot t$, which was already being grown by the beginning of the Old Kingdom,[2] but was, on the contrary, the primitive $bd \cdot t$. Thus, he was patron-god of the month of the festival $\check{S}f\text{-}bd \cdot t$, a name which probably means 'The Swelling of the $bd \cdot t$',[3] and similarly it was a sheaf of $bd \cdot t$ that Ramesses II and III reaped ceremonially before him.[4] $Bd \cdot t$ was the emmer-wheat, *triticum dicoccum*[5] of Fayyumi, Merimdian, Badarian, Gerzean[6] and Maadian days.[7] Like Seth, Min clearly goes back to the dawn of civilization in the Egyptian world.

Merimdah and the Fayyum lie on the Libyan side of Egypt, on the edge of the Sahara. There is a remarkable

[1] Wainwright in *JEA*, xvii, p. 185. In the 50's of the Sequence Dating, cf. Petrie, *Prehistoric Egypt*, Pl. xxiii, 31, 32, and pp. 19, 20.

[2] A granary marked as being filled with $sw \cdot t$ is shown in the Third Dynasty, Murray, *Saqqara Mastabas*, i, Pl. ii, centre bottom, and p. 36, and again under Khufu, Junker, *Giza*, i, fig. 31. Actual specimens of a better quality wheat than emmer have been found in tombs of the late Old Kingdom and of the Twelfth Dynasty, A. Schulz, *Die Getreide der alten Aegypter*, pp. 18, 19, 23 (published in *Abhandl. der Natur-forschenden Gesells. zu Halle*, Neue Folge, No. 5, 1916), though what its name may have been is quite uncertain.

[3] Meyer, *Nachträge zur äg. Chronologie* (published in *Abhandl. k. preuss. Ak. der Wiss.* 1907), Table facing p. 16. Cf. Gauthier, *Les fêtes du dieu Min*, pp. 3–5.

[4] RAMESSES II, L. *D.* iii, Pl. 162; RAMESSES III, L. *D.* iii, Pl. 212, b.

[5] Gauthier, *op. cit.* pp. 5–7, 289, and Keimer's communication, p. 95. Murray in *Ancient Egypt*, 1929, p. 45 and figs. 8–13. Unfortunately Gauthier calls it *épeautre*, 'spelt', all through his publication.

[6] Caton-Thompson and Gardner, *The Desert Fayum*, pp. 47, 48; Junker in *Anzeiger*, 1929, p. 214; 1930, p. 44, note 2. It is perhaps worth noting that it, 'barley', does not seem to be connected with Min, though it was grown by the Fayyumis along with emmer-wheat. At Merimdah a vetch was also grown with the emmer-wheat.

[7] Menghin and Amer, *Excavations...at Maadi*, p. 52.

spell in the Pyramid Texts, which has been called in evidence already in the course of these studies (*JEA*, XVIII, pp. 164, 171), and will be of importance to our argument again, pp. 26, 27 *infra*. Among other things it tells of Seth's death, refers to fertility activities, and in §§ 1456 ff. has to do with Libya. From the Twenty-Second Dynasty at any rate Seth was an important god in the Oases of the western desert,[1] and his relative Ꜣꞩ had been 'Lord of Libya' in the Fifth Dynasty.[2] 'Lord of the West' was the title of *Ḥꜣ*, the Mountain-god,[3] who is likely to have belonged to the sky-religion.[4] The sky-god Amûn is not unlike Seth,[5] and like him was, or became, important in Libya. His name seems to be Libyan, for in that language *amân* means 'water'.[6] The stars must figure large to those who in a clear atmosphere think about the sky, and of them the Imperishable Stars were peculiarly important to the Egyptians. The chief of these was the constellation of the Great Bear and it belonged to Seth.[7] The passage in the Pyramid Texts about Seth's death also mentions the Imperishable Stars, and in §§ 1456–8 repeats the statement three times that they 'travel through Libya'. In keeping with all this is its reference to the time before Seth had quarrelled with Horus,

---

[1] Gardiner in *JEA*, XIX, pp. 21, 22 = Spiegelberg in *Rec. de Trav.* XXI, pp. 16 ff.; Roeder in Roscher, *Lexikon*, s.v. *Set*, col. 732; Kees in Pauly-Wissowa, *Real-Encyclopädie*, s.v. *Seth*, col. 1904. In the Twenty-Ninth Dynasty a chieftain of Siwah was named after him, Sethardus, 'Seth it is who hath given him', Steindorff in *ZÄS*, LXIX, p. 22.

[2] Borchardt, *Das Grabdenkmal des Königs Saꜣḥureꜥ*, II, Pl. I.

[3] *Anns. Serv.* XVI, pp. 71, 76; L. D. III, Pl. 69, e; V. Schmidt, *Ny Carlsberg Glyptotek: Den aeg. Samling* (1908), pp. 201, 204; Piehl, *Inscr. hiérogl.* Seconde Série, Pl. lxxvi, 9; Brugsch, *Rec. de mons. égyptiens*, V, Pl. xlvi, ll. 2, 3; id. *Dict. géogr.* p. 1291; cf. also Kees, *Horus und Seth*, I, pp. 24, 25.   [4] Wainwright in *JEA*, XXI, pp. 161, 162.

[5] Id. in *op. cit.* XX, pp. 147–50.

[6] Möller in *OLZ*, 1921, col. 194; Wainwright in *JEA*, XX, p. 146.

[7] Wainwright in Griffith, *Studies*, p. 375.

§ 1463, i.e. before the dawn of history. Thus, not only does the sky-religion in Egypt show itself to be extremely ancient, but also to be especially connected with the west, with Libya, with the Sahara.

The main outlines of such religions as this earliest of Egyptian ones are well known, whether in mediaeval Europe or in modern Africa. As pointed out above, the system centres in the person of the god, or the king who acts for him here below, who controls the weather and hence the fertility of the earth.

Nothing is more certain than that the Pharaoh was divine. He was occasionally called 𓅓𓊹, 'The Great God',[1] as representative here on earth of the primitive nameless sky-god who was later fused with Horus.[2] Later, when he had changed his religion to sun-worship, he continued the idea of his divinity by becoming 'Son of the Sun', and all through history his regular title was 𓅓𓊹, 'The Good God'. At least one Pharaoh claimed power over the elements, as would be suitable to the earthly incarnation of the sky-god. The Great Chief of the Hittites is represented as writing to the chief of Kedi that Ramesses II 'giveth breath to whom he will.... If the god receive not his offering, it (the Land of the Hittites) beholdeth not the rain of heaven'.[3] Elsewhere the Hittite king is made to say 'Our Lord Sutekh is angry with us, the sky no longer gives water upon us', upon which he proceeds to send presents and even his daughter to Ramesses II 'that he may grant us peace that we may

---

[1] E.g. Sneferu, Khufu, Sahurê, Neuserrê, Pepi; Gardiner and Peet, *The Inscriptions of Sinai*, Pls. ii, 5, ii, 7=iii, 7 left, v, vi, viii, 16; Ramesses II, Roeder in *ZÄS*, LXI, p. 62.

[2] Junker, *Giza*, II, p. 51, and cf. p. 9 *supra*.

[3] Erman, *The Literature of the Ancient Egyptians* (trans. Blackman), p. 271. Another papyrus gives the same passage, Gardiner in *JEA*, V, p. 188.

live'.[1] Then Ramesses deliberated about the comfort of the escort he had sent to meet the Hittites 'during these days of rain and snow which come in winter'.[2] He, therefore, sacrificed to his father Sutekh praying '[Thou canst stop] the rain and the north wind and the snow'.[3] The result was that 'his father Sutekh heard all his prayers: the sky became calm, summer days arrived'.[4] The Hittites were astonished and said 'The Land of the Hittites is his (Ramesses II's) like Egypt, and even (?) the sky: it is under his seal (orders) and does everything that he wishes'.[5] It is noticeable that Ramesses II was thought to have influence with Sutekh, Seth the storm-god, and that he belonged to the Nineteenth Dynasty, when there was a great recrudescence of Seth-worship. Hatshepsut sacrificed to Hathor, Mistress of Punt, 'that she may bring wind' on the departure of her fleet for that land.[6] Tethmosy IV, Amenhotep III and Akhenaton each calls himself the 'Lord of the sweet breeze'.[7] A regular boon desired of the Pharaoh was 'the breath of life', which no doubt referred to the same idea. There can be no doubt, therefore, that power in the air was ascribed, at least sometimes, to the divine Pharaohs.[8]

Kings of this type contain within themselves the power

---

[1] Kuentz in *Anns. Serv.* xxv, p. 212, ll. 31, 32 = p. 231.

[2] Id. *op. cit.* p. 215, ll. 36, 37 = p. 232.

[3] Id. *op. cit.* p. 216, l. 37 = p. 233.

[4] Id. *op. cit.* p. 216, l. 38 = p. 234.

[5] Id. *op. cit.* p. 221, top half = p. 234, l. 41.

[6] B. *A.R.* ii, § 252. It might be argued that this was only taking ordinary precautions, for in the Eleventh Dynasty a mere official, Henu, had sacrificed on the departure of the fleet he had built, id. *op. cit.* i, § 432. However, the private individual's sacrifice had apparently been for good luck in general, for he does not ask any special boon, whether of fine weather or favourable winds.

[7] Drioton in *Egyptian Religion* (New York), 1933, p. 41.

[8] It could hardly be expected that so exalted a personage as the Pharaoh should not be able to control the elements, seeing that the

that produces prosperity. An unusually clear case is that of the divine king of the Jukun in Nigeria. He is expected to control the rains and the wind,[1] and is himself the well-being of his people. At his installation he is addressed thus: 'The whole world is yours. You are our guinea-corn and beans our *jô* and our *aku* (i.e. the spirits and gods of our worship), etc., etc.' Then, when he is presented to the people, 'All then fall down before their new sovereign, and throw dust on their heads, saying, "Our crops", "our rain", "our health", and "our wealth"'.[2] The same sentiments are expressed by the courtiers in their address to Ramesses II.[3] They say: 'We come to thee; Lord of the Sky; Lord of the Earth; Rê, Life of the Earth in its entirety, Lord of the life-period, Long of life; Atum to the unknown ones (?); Lord of destiny, creating the plenteous harvest; Khnum, fashioning the people, Giving breath to the nostrils of all people, Causing the entire Ennead of the Gods to live; Pillar of the Sky; Beam (support) of the Earth; Leader who directeth the two banks of the Nile; Lord of many provisions and abundance of corn, there is a plenteous harvest wherever his sandals may be; Making great men, fashioning small men, whose words created provisions; August Lord, watchful while all men sleep, whose strength hath protected Egypt; Strong in foreign lands, who cometh back after triumphing, whose strong arm protecteth Egypt; Beloved of Maat (Goddess of Truth), who liveth by her through his

ordinary magico-medical practitioner expected the gods to believe him, when he threatened 'If he hear not [my words], I will [not] allow the sun to rise, [I will not] allow the Nile to flow' (Twentieth Dynasty), Gardiner, *Hieratic Papyri in the British Museum*, 3rd Series, Chester Beatty Gift, vol. I, Text, p. 65.

[1] C. K. Meek, *A Sudanese Kingdom*, p. 130.
[2] Id. *op. cit.* p. 137.
[3] Mariette, *Abydos*, I, Pl. vi, ll. 36–40 = Maspero, *L'inscription dédicatoire du temple d'Abydos*, pp. 23 ff. = Gauthier in *ZÄS*, XLVIII, p. 56.

laws; Protecting the two banks of the Nile; Rich in years; Greatly victorious; He whose terror hath crushed foreign lands; Our King; Our Lord; Our Sun; Atum liveth when speaking through his mouth. Behold us here before thy Majesty; Mayest thou decree to us the life which thou givest; Pharaoh—may he live prosperous and hale—is the Breath of our nostrils, and all men live when he shineth for them.' This is no mere jumble of fantastic hyperbole and bombast for a king of overweening pride. It is on the contrary a very complete enumeration of the qualities of a divine fertility-king, such as the Jukun king is in Nigeria, and in Egypt such as Ramesses II shows himself, and the divine Nitocris was believed, to have been (pp. 41, 45). Besides the description of the king's duties and activities, he is said to enact the parts of Rê, Atum, and Khnum. The immediate interest to us here is that he is Lord of the Sky and Lord of the Earth; he is actually the Pillar supporting the sky and the Beam supporting the earth;[1] the Life of the whole earth, giving life to everything and the breath (of life) to all people, even being the very 'Breath of our nostrils',[2] himself living safely, long, and healthily; the divine power within the Pharaoh produces abundance with plenteous harvests;[3] he crowns the prosperity of his reign by making

---

[1] Cf. *JEA*, xxi, p. 168, for the 'great *wḥ* which beginnest in Heaven [and reachest to] the Underworld'. The Berbers call the Milky Way *Ajgu n tignau*, 'The Beam of the Sky', Hastings, *Encyclopaedia of Religion and Ethics*, ii, p. 510.

[2] In Lamentations iv, 20 the king is spoken of in the identical words: 'The breath of our nostrils.'

[3] The expression 'there is a plenteous harvest wherever his sandals may be' is specially interesting as carrying back to this age the idea of the shoe as a fertility-symbol. Herodotus, ii, 91, records that on the appearance of Perseus' sandal at Min's city of Panopolis all Egypt was accustomed to flourish. Sartori has collected other cases in *Zeits. des Vereins für Volkskunde*, 1894, pp. 44–8, 50–4. Perseus was a sky-god, *JEA*, xxi, pp. 156, 157.

his people victorious over their enemies. To do all this a divine fertility-king must keep himself in good health and live a well-ordered life. For as he functions regularly and in good order, so will the universe remain stable and continue in its allotted course, for he himself is the universe.

The service rendered by such kings has always been to ensure the fruitfulness of the earth, and consequent health of the people. Hence, it is natural to find them curing the sick and playing their part in the labours of the field. It was demanded of at least one ruler of Egypt, Vespasian, that he should keep the people in health.[1] Though he ridiculed the idea, he was induced to cure two invalids, by spitting on the eyes of the blind man and by touching the diseased hand of the other with his heel.[2] In Archaic days a Pharaoh is seen hoeing the ground, perhaps for sowing,[3] and this he does in the presence of the ancient sky- and fertility-gods Seth (twice), Min, and Ḥꜣ. Of these Ḥꜣ at least is Libyan, as has already been pointed out. Originally the same carving

---

[1] In England kings were expected to do the same at least as late as the early eighteenth century. William III was only persuaded to do so once, and then he accompanied his magic touch with the remark 'God give you better health and more sense', Frazer, *The Magic Art*, I, pp. 368–71. For a study of the whole subject see M. Bloch, *Les rois thaumaturges* (*Publications de la faculté des lettres de l'Université de Strasbourg*, Fasc. 19).

[2] Tacitus, *Hist.* IV, 81; Suetonius, *Divus Vespasianus*, § 7. Similarly 'the King of the Jews' cured blind men with his spittle, Mark viii, 23; John ix, 6. By putting his foot on the other invalid Vespasian would have made use of his sandal, which, as has been seen, brings prosperity.

[3] Quibell and Petrie, *Hierakonpolis*, I, Pl. xxvi, C, 4 and p. 9. The symbols of the gods appear along with others in the top row in fig. I of this plate. As Petrie suggests, he might be attending to the irrigation dykes. On the other hand ploughing and sowing in Egypt take place on the sodden land, as soon as it appears from the waters of the inundation. This would account for the water in the scene, and the attendant seems to be spilling something, as it might be seeds, from his basket rather than having it filled with earth.

also represented a harvest scene of which nothing now remains but the hands of a man holding a great sheaf of corn.[1] In the New Kingdom both Ramesses II and Ramesses III ceremonially reaped a sheaf of corn with a gold-inlaid sickle.[2] This they both did before Min, who had been present at the hoeing ceremony of Archaic days. The antiquity of the harvest festival is further established by two

Archaic Pharaoh hoeing the earth

Ramesses III ceremonially reaping a sheaf of *bd·t*.

facts. First, the corn so reaped was laid not so much before the anthropomorphic Min as before his bull; secondly, it was not the good wheat *sw·t* that had been grown in Egypt long before the New Kingdom, but the old *bd·t* of Fayyumi days.[3]

Yet, again, the king carried out the well-known *sed-*

---

[1] Id. *loc. cit.* fig. 6.

[2] RAMESSES II, L. *D.* III, Pl. 162; RAMESSES III, L. *D.* III, Pl. 212, b. At Karnak Ramesses II again reaps a sheaf of corn, which looks like *bd·t*, before Min. It is presented to him by an anthropomorphized ankh, the sign of life, Burton MSS. 25638,35 Porter and Moss, *Topographical Bibliography*, II, p. 47, no. 10.

[3] See p. 12.

2-2

festival. A great deal has been written about this, but almost always under the belief that it was an Osiris-festival.[1] The present writer would point out that in its origin the festival cannot be Osirian, for among other things it long antedates the appearance of Osiris.[2] Among all those who have studied the question Petrie, *Ancient Egypt*, 1925, pp. 65 ff., seems to be the only one who has recognized the *sed* as a ceremony to ensure the fertility of the fields. Something of the sort it certainly was in its oldest and simplest form, though in the process of time it seems to have become more complex.

Its name *sed* (𓋴𓊃) shows by its determinative that it was connected with the land.[3] It consisted essentially in a running ceremony, performed in Archaic days before the king[4] and from the First Dynasty onwards by the king

---

[1] For example, Kees, *Opfertanz*, pp. 160 ff., 190, 191, 248; Moret, *Mystères égyptiens*, p. 68; id. *Du caractère religieux*, pp. 263, 264; Moret and Davy, *From Tribe to Empire*, pp. 151, 153; Moret, *The Nile and Egyptian Civilization*, pp. 130 ff.; id. *La mise à mort du dieu en Égypte*, p. 51; Murray in *Man*, 1914, pp. 17–23. On the other hand a connexion with Osiris has been denied, and rightly so far as the present writer can see, by Gardiner in *JEA*, II, p. 124, and Newberry, *Reports of the British Association for the Advancement of Science*, 1923 (*Egypt as a Field for Anthropological Research*), p. 185, or more conveniently in Roeder's translation in *Der Alte Orient*, XXVII, p. 21. Kees, *op. cit.* p. 165, also questions the supposed identity of the *sed*-robe with that of Osiris. Kees has studied the *sed*-festival again more recently, but confines himself mostly to the order of the ceremonies and comparison of one scene with another, *Re-Heiligtum*, III.

[2] Osiris took the place of the Anzety; does not appear before the end of the Fifth Dynasty, when he begins to creep into the Pyramid Texts; does not enter into his full vigour until the Middle Kingdom. Hence, if the *sed*-robe be really the same as that of Osiris, it would seem that Osiris was dressed as an ancient king and not, as is generally thought, that the king was dressed as Osiris.

[3] It is not the tail sign, as has so often been thought, but that for land, *Wb. d. aeg. Spr.* IV, p. 364, s.v.

[4] Quibell and Petrie, *Hierakonpolis*, I, Pl. xxvi, B.

himself.[1] In this he is encouraged by a man who beckons him on with the words ⟨glyph⟩,[2] which Kees would read 'Come! Bring!!'[3] and Sethe 'The Bringer cometh!'[4] The ceremony is stated many times to be concerned with the fields.[5] In the early Eighteenth Dynasty besides running with the flail the king runs up with vases of water.[6] The *sed*-festival belongs to the old sky- and fertility-religion, Min-Amûn being especially prominent.[7] The Archaic scene shows the two fans ⟨glyph⟩, and by the Fifth Dynasty the symbol ⟨glyph⟩ is shown. Both of these represent Min-Amûn, the second

[1] Petrie, *Royal Tombs*, I, Pl. xv, 16; Firth and Quibell, *The Step Pyramid*, Pl. 42; Bissing and Kees, *Re-Heiligtum*, II, Pls. 13, 14, figs. 33 b, 34. A belief has grown up that the royal children in their palanquins were women and princesses. So far as the present writer sees they are always men, wearing the short hair of men, Quibell and Petrie, *Hierakonpolis*, I, Pl. xxvi, B; Bissing and Kees, *op. cit.* III, Pl. xiv, 246 and pp. 35, 36; Petrie, *The Palace of Apries*, Pl. ii, 6 = iv; id. *Meydum and Memphis*, III, Pl. xxxi, top; Möller in *ZÄS*, xxxix, Pl. iv, where they are transformed into the male gods, Imsety, Hapi, and Duamutef. The figures on Bissing and Kees, *op. cit.* II, Pl. xviii, 44, d are too damaged to be helpful, and it is impossible to pronounce on the 'children's' sex on the third mace from *Hierakonpolis*, I, Pl. xxvi, C, 2. Kees points out that in Neuserrê's case the princess is present, is labelled 'The Royal Daughter', and walks behind the three men, who are also there in their usual palanquins, *Re-Heiligtum*, III, p. 36 = II, Pl. 3, fig. 7 b.

[2] Bissing and Kees, *Re-Heiligtum*, II, Pls. 13, 14, figs. 33, b, 34. The remains of the second are visible in each case. At this date it is men who encourage him, not *mert*-goddesses as usual.

[3] *Opfertanz*, p. 104.

[4] Sethe in Borchardt, *Das Grabdenkmal des Königs Saʒhureᶜ*, II, p. 102.

[5] *Loc. cit.* There is no need to suppose with Kees, *Opfertanz*, pp. 158–60, that *šḫt* refers to sceptres. In fact he himself seems to have given up the idea, *Nachrichten von der Gesells. der Wiss. zu Göttingen, Phil.-hist. Klasse*, 1929, p. 59.

[6] Kees, *Opfertanz*, pp. 22 ff.

[7] Kees, *Re-Heiligtum*, III, Pl. 31, fig. 482 and p. 29, but not Pl. 10, fig. 197, which Kees also takes to be Min.

being 'the waters of heaven',[1] and the late coffin, where the ceremony is performed for Osiris, shows the whole shrine of Min.[2] By the Third Dynasty the door-pivots are introduced representing the depths of heaven or possibly even the caverns of the Nile.[3] Until the Eleventh Dynasty the king only carries the flail in these running scenes, and that as is well known belongs to Min,[4] and is given to such sky-gods as the mummified hawk of Letopolis 𓅓[5] and the *wḥ*.[6] Ancient as is our earliest scene, it is evident that the festival goes back much further still. Nekheb (Eileithyiapolis, el Kab) was the city of Nekhebt, the southern patroness of the kingship. Nekhen (Hieraconpolis) just across the river formed a pair with it, and the Souls of Nekhen represent the prehistoric kings of Upper Egypt. In the Archaic scene the enthroned king is protected by the vulture of Nekhebt, although he is seated there as king of Lower Egypt, and in the Fifth Dynasty scene the priest of the prehistoric Souls of Nekhen plays the leading part after the king himself. He acts as standard bearer, meeting the king, conducting him to the place of running, and actually running the course with him. Several of the old sky-gods figure at the ceremony. It has just been shown that Min was prominent. The shrine of the primitive mummified hawk of the Thunderbolt-city, Letopolis, was visited by Zoser at his *sed*-festival in the Third

---

[1] *JEA*, xx, pp. 145, 146.

[2] Möller in *ZÄS*, xxxix, Pl. iv.

[3] Firth and Quibell, *loc. cit.*; Wainwright in *JEA*, xx, p. 146.

[4] Petrie in *Ancient Egypt*, 1925, p. 68 and the tabulation p. 69. It was probably the flail that the archaic statues of Min carried in the right hand, which is bored to receive something, Capart, *Primitive Art in Egypt*, fig. 166.

[5] Firth and Quibell, *The Step Pyramid*, Pl. 41 and p. 60; Sethe, *Pyr.* §§ 771, 1211, 1670, 1864, 2015, 2086.

[6] Though not before the Twelfth Dynasty, Blackman, *Meir*, I, p. 4.

Dynasty,[1] and this god's successor, Horus Khenty-Khem, still appears at Osorkon's in the Twenty-Second Dynasty.[2]

The almost unknown ⚒, Double-axe god, is to be found at Neuserrê's sed-festival,[3] as is the Sky-pole, _wḫ_.[4] _Ḥꜣ_, the Mountain-god of the West, was another little known sky-god, and his name occurs at Neuserrê's sed-festival.[5] He purifies Hatshepsut for the 'making of the sed-festival very often like Rê for ever'.[6] He and his priest are present at Osorkon's sed-festival,[7] as he is at those of Neos Dionysos[8] and Tiberius.[9]

The ceremony clearly went back at least into Prehistoric times. But it was still more ancient than that, even going back to Libyan days.[10] It has just been seen that _Ḥꜣ_ was concerned with it, and he was god of the West (p. 13), god of Manu the western mountain, etc.[11] Hence it is natural to find Libya (_Ṯḥnw_) playing a large part. The tablet of Udymu in the First Dynasty shows the running ceremony and names Libya (Fig. on p. 72).[12] In the Third Dynasty

---

[1] Firth and Quibell, _The Step Pyramid_, Pl. 41 and p. 60; Kees in _Nachrichten von der Gesells. der Wiss. zu Göttingen_, Phil.-hist. Klasse, 1929, pp. 58, 59.

[2] Naville, _The Festival Hall of Osorkon_, II, Pl. vii, bottom row.

[3] Bissing and Kees, _Re-Heiligtum_, II, Pl. 19, No. 45, b, top row.

[4] Id. _op. cit._ III, p. 50 and Pl. 32, No. 501. That it was a sky-pole and was represented by a bull, see Wainwright in _JEA_, XXI, p. 168.

[5] Bissing and Kees, _op. cit._ III, Pl. 10, No. 207 and p. 29.

[6] Naville, _Deir el Bahari_, Pl. lxiii.

[7] Id. _The Festival Hall_, Pls. ii, 8; xii, 7.

[8] L. D. IV, Pl. 52, a.   [9] L. D. IV, Pl. 74, c.

[10] After having put together this paragraph, I was happy to find that Newberry also believes the _sed_ to be of Libyan origin, _Reports of the British Association_, 1923, p. 185, or more conveniently in Roeder's translation in _Der alte Orient_, XXVII, p. 21.

[11] E.g. L. D. IV, Pl. 74 c.

[12] Petrie, _Royal Tombs_, I, Pl. xv, 16 = Fig. on p. 72, _infra_.

Zoser wears the Libyan penistasche when he is running.[1] A man representing Libya assists at Neuserrê's running ceremony, where he is labelled) o, *Ṯḥnw*, Libya.[2] Neith of Libya attends the festival,[3] and the chapel of Horus of Libya figures elsewhere at it.[4] The priest of Horus of Libya holds the great *wȝś*-sceptre at Neuserrê's festival,[5] and at Tethmosy III's Horus of Libya himself presents it to the king.[6] 'Horus of Libya before the *sed*' is one of the many gods represented at Osorkon's festival.[7] It is also said to this king: 'Thou appearest upon the throne of Horus, in order that thou mayest overthrow Libya.'[8] At his *sed*-festival Mentuhotep I smites a chieftain of Libya.[9]

Physical activity is an essential in fertility-rites such as these clearly were. No doubt the king's agility here brought fertility to the fields, and induced the necessary activity of the skies in providing the water required. However, even our earliest records come from a time when the Egyptians had left Libya, and were no longer dependent on the rain for their crops, but on the Nile. Hence, Den-Udymu records on his *sed*-tablet what seems to be a record of letting the

---

[1] Firth and Quibell, *The Step Pyramid*, Pl. 42 and p. 60. The detail is more distinct in *Anns. Serv.* xxvii, Pl. iii to Firth's article, pp. 105 ff.

[2] Bissing and Kees, *Re-Heiligtum*, ii, Pl. 13, fig. 33, b.

[3] Id. *op. cit.* Pl. 7, fig. 17, and Kees in iii, p. 9.

[4] Bissing and Kees, *op. cit.* Pl. 16, fig. 39, middle of the lower register.   [5] Id. *op. cit.* Pl. 16, fig. 39, lower register.

[6] Id. *op. cit.* iii, p. 11, and Beiblatt A, lower register. It was with their closely allied *ḏᶜm*-sceptres that the Imperishable Stars travelled through Libya, Sethe, *Pyr.* §§ 1456–8. Cf. Wainwright in *JEA*, xviii, p. 164.

[7] Naville, *Festival Hall*, Pl. vii, end of bottom row.

[8] Id. *op. cit.* Pl. xvii, 11. Cf. Udymu's above-mentioned inscription, which names both Libya and 'Seizing the throne of Horus'.

[9] Bissing-Bruckmann, *Denkmäler*, Pl. 33, A, b (in Lieferung 6), and Bissing's discussion, though he does not realize that the 'pivots' and standards show it to be a *sed*-festival. The plate is reproduced by Naville with his article in *Rec. de Trav.* xxxii, pp. 52 ff.

inundation into the irrigation basins (Fig. on p. 72).[1] It is evident, therefore, that the Pharaoh was concerned with the welfare of the crops. It was with good reason that it was the Pharaoh who received the revelation of the prospects, first for the cattle and then for the crops in Genesis xli, 1–7.

Thus we find that the Pharaohs were divine; controlled the activities of the sky; kept their people in health; hoed the ground; reaped the harvest; carried out a ceremony for the fertility of the fields, and concerned themselves with the opening of the dykes for the inundation. Hence, it is already clear that they had many of the duties well known as those of the religion which, in Europe at least, goes back to palaeo-lithic days. The Pharaohs were in fact fertility-kings, upon whose own health and proper observance of the rites the health and wealth of the country depended. To those familiar with the sort of routine incumbent upon such kings[2] it is evident that Diodorus (1, 70, 71) is labouring this point in his long discussion of the duties of the Pharaohs. He says, for instance, that 'not only the order of the priests but, in short, all the inhabitants of Egypt were less concerned for their wives and children and their other cherished posses-sions than for the safety of their kings'. 'But all their (the kings') acts were regulated by prescriptions set forth in laws, not only their administrative acts, but also those that had to do with the way in which they spent their time from day to day, and with the food which they ate.' 'And the hours of both the day and night were laid out according to a plan, and at the specified hours it was absolutely required of the

---

[1] The group may well mean 'Opening the gate of the waters', i.e. cutting the dam.

[2] See for instance Frazer, *Taboo and the Perils of the Soul*, pp. 1 ff.

king that he should do what the laws stipulated and not what he thought best.' 'For there was a set time not only for his holding audiences or rendering judgments, but even for his taking a walk, bathing, and sleeping with his wife, and, in a word, for every act of his life.'

It has already been stated that the last duty of such fertility-kings, as the Egyptian prove to have been, is to lay down their lives at the proper time for the good of their people. To show that the Pharaoh also owed, or had owed, this duty to his country, and to point out some of its effects on Egyptian religion, history and folk-lore form a large part of the rest of the present study. In following out this theme much more evidence comes to light that the Pharaohs were indeed fertility-kings, and that the sky-religion and its practices were ancient and account for much that has hitherto been obscure.

Dr Margaret A. Murray has already called attention in *Ancient Egypt*, 1928, pp. 8 ff., to a pair of remarkable spells, Nos. 570, 571, in the Pyramid Texts. They give some details of the death to which the sky-god Seth, and the Pharaoh, his representative here on earth, were liable and of their escape from it. The translations here given have been kindly supplied by Mr Faulkner, and they practically speak for themselves.[1] The first begins in § 1443 with 'Utterance; The face of the sky is washed, the (celestial) vault is bright', clearly referring to the appearance of the sky after rain. The spell is thus concerned with the weather. Further on, in §§ 1453–5, it is said that 'Pepi hath escaped his day of death even as Seth escaped his day of death; Pepi hath escaped the half months of death even as Seth escaped his half months of death; Pepi hath escaped his months of death even as

---

[1] In justice to Mr Faulkner it should be noted here that he finds much in these passages that is obscure.

Seth escaped his months of death; Pepi hath escaped the year of death even as Seth escaped his year of death. Do not plough the earth (??) Oh ye hands of Pepi which support Nut as Shu, even the bones of Pepi which are of iron (?) and his members which know not destruction, for Pepi is a star which illumineth the sky. Ascend thou to this Pepi, Oh god, that he may be protected (?), so that neither heaven nor earth may be void of this Pepi for ever.' Spell 571 makes further reference to the deaths of Seth and the king, and to the possibility of their escape. In §§ 1467-9 it says: 'This Pepi escapeth the day of death even as Seth escaped his day of death; this Pepi is at your *wdrw*, Oh ye gods of the nether sky, who cannot perish (?) through their foes, this Pepi perisheth (?) not through his foes; who die not through a king, this Pepi dieth not through a king; who die not through any death, this Pepi dieth not through any death; Pepi is an Imperishable Star, the great. . . of heaven in the midst of the Scorpion (?)-House. Rê hath taken for himself this Pepi to heaven that this Pepi may live as he liveth who entereth into the west of the sky and ascendeth from the east of the sky.'

The words refer of course to the king in the next world, but naturally the similes are taken from this. For some reason not stated both the sky-god Seth and the king, his representative here on earth, were subject to death at certain fixed periods. Equally it was possible for them to avoid it. It is at least remarkable for the present study that this should be followed by instructions to the king about ploughing the earth, and that for this he should be likened to Shu, the air-god who supports the sky, Nut.[1] On this occasion the

---

[1] Compare the Mock King, the 'Lord of the Heavenly Hosts' in Siam, p. 3. He clearly represents the sky-god and ploughs the nine ritual furrows.

king is instructed not to plough the earth, though an archaic king has just been seen in what is probably this very act— hoeing, however, not ploughing as here. It should also be noted that besides discussing the death of Seth and the king, their escape, and ploughing the earth, Spell 570 speaks of very ancient days, the time before Horus had fought with Seth (§ 1463). It also includes a reference to Libya, and to the activities there of those Imperishable Stars (§§ 1456 ff.) which were so important a feature of the sky to the Pharaonic Egyptians.

Spell 571 states once more that Seth and the king escape from their day of death. It then goes on to speak of the king's escape from death through his foes, through a king, or through any form of death. Besides death from his foes the only other form of death specified is contained in the statement that 'this Pepi dieth not through a king'.[1] This of course need be nothing more than an elaboration of the aforementioned foes. It would then merely mean that Pepi shall never be taken prisoner in warfare and executed by a rival king. But in the light of what is to come, and the milieu in which this sentence occurs, does not this mean something else? Are not two different forms of death mentioned here; one at the hands of enemies, the other at the hands of a king, who in this case would be something other than an enemy? If so, it might well mean that Pepi had no intention of being sacrificed, as at one time he lawfully might have been, by his successor. This fate for a king has been common enough in the world, a few examples of which have

---

[1] If further research were to establish Dr Margaret Murray's quite possible reading of *nyswt* as 'kingship' rather than 'king' (*Ancient Egypt*, 1928, p. 8) the meaning would be clearer still. The passage would then read 'who die not on account of the kingship, this Pepi dieth not on account of the kingship'.

been quoted on p. 5. In Egypt it will be seen that Bocchoris was actually sacrificed by his successor (p. 39), and that in story Sesostris' would-be successor attempted to do the same to him (p. 48). But Sesostris escaped like Seth and Abu Nerûz his modern survival, and, again like Seth and Abu Nerûz (pp. 59, 60), the death prepared for both Sesostris and Bocchoris was by fire.

The hoeing of the earth was probably a mystical act. As has just been seen Pepi was instructed not to plough the earth and elsewhere, § 693, another Hoer of the Earth is also told not to do so, but to protect himself from his enemies. It was also an act of cosmic importance, for on another occasion, § 1120, it takes place to the accompaniment of the speaking of the sky, trembling of the earth, roaring of the two nomes of the god, etc., while the dead Pharaoh mounts to heaven.[1] In § 1394 much the same happens when he descends to earth. At any rate it was much more than a mere agricultural process, for offerings were made when the earth was hoed, §§ 817, 1394, 1561. In the mid-Eighteenth Dynasty there were at least two Festivals of Hoeing the Earth. At _Ddw_, which was known to the Greeks as Busiris, there took place 'The Great Hoeing of the Earth in Busiris, on that night when the earth is hoed with their (Osiris' enemies, i.e. the Companions of Seth) blood'. The gloss elaborates this and says: 'The Companions of Seth came and changed themselves into goats; then were they slaughtered before these gods, and their blood which flowed from them was _ndr_.'[2] The same papyrus names another Festival

---

[1] Cf. § 1561. Of course the commotion may have been due to the Pharaoh's going to heaven, not to the hoeing.

[2] Grapow, _Religiöse Urkunden_, II, pp. 127, 128, Abschnitt 8 of ch. xviii of the Book of the Dead. The _dd_-pillar, which was the fetish at _Ddw_-Busiris, originally represented Seth, Sethe, _Dramatische Texte_, pp. 153–60 (published as _Untersuchungen_, x), and it is not until the New King-

of Hoeing the Earth, which took place at Heracleopolis.[1] Similarly, in the early Nineteenth Dynasty there was a 'hoeing of blood which came forth from Heracleopolis', and this may have been Seth's, for he is mentioned in the previous line.[2] Evidently the people took part in the Heracleopolitan festival, for in the Eighteenth Dynasty Nu says: 'I am seizing a hoe on the Day of Hoeing the Earth in Heracleopolis.'[3] The mixing of the blood of the storm-god with the soil is comparable to the practices of many peoples,[4] and without doubt was intended to promote its fertility. Both ceremonies bear in themselves a mark of primitiveness, for they employed a hoe down to the end, although the plough had been in use at least as early as the Third Dynasty.[5] Another point of interest is that one of the cities where the festival was celebrated was Heracleopolis. This city will be encountered again (p. 36), and then as a stronghold of Libyanism.

dom that we have clear evidence of its representing Osiris, Schäfer in Griffith, *Studies*, p. 430.

[1] Naville, *Das aegyptische Todtenbuch*, i, ch. xx, ll. 7, 8, at Neref, the cemetery of Heracleopolis. The text goes back to the Middle Kingdom, when, however, no place is given. In Saitic times another version of this chapter says the hoeing festival took place at *Ḍdw*-Busiris, Grapow, *Religiöse Urkunden*, p. 106, Abschnitt 8 of ch. xx of the Book of the Dead.

[2] Naville, *Das aegyptische Todtenbuch*, i, ch. clxxv, ll. 31, 32.

[3] Budge, *Facsimiles of the Papyri of Hunefer, etc.: Nu.*, Pl. vii, ch. i, l. 15. Again in the Nineteenth Dynasty, id. *Facsimile of the Papyrus of Ani*, Pl. v, ch. i, ll. 29, 30; Naville, *Das aegyptische Todtenbuch*, ii, p. 11, Ag, l. 22.

[4] In Zululand when the old rain-chief was killed his blood was mixed with the seed-corn to increase its fertility, Seligman, *Egypt and Negro Africa*, p. 31. Similarly at the time of sowing the fields the Dinka rainmaker mixes the fat of the sacrifice with the seed-corn, which is distributed to the people, id. *op. cit.* p. 26.

[5] Petrie, *Medum*, Pl. xii. Cf. also Pl. xxviii, 4 and *JEA*, xxiii, Pl. iv.

Seth sacrifices clearly took place with a view to fertilizing the earth, and in the beginning the ruler had played the part of the god. A remarkable and hitherto unparalleled text has just been published by Gardiner,[1] and though terribly fragmentary a good deal may be gleaned from it. Among other things it shows that as late as the Nineteenth Dynasty a section of the Egyptians were known to be 'Followers of Seth', Typhonians, by certain marks and characteristics.[2] Of such it is said: 'The god in him is Seth', and he declares himself on at least one occasion by the redness of his devotee's eyes. Another badly damaged sentence mentions a 'red man' and his hair.[3] The different categories of Typhonians had special spans of life allotted to them, some eighty-four years, others sixty, yet others a period now lost, and of another it is said: 'His lifetime is (that of) Seth....' The manner of the death of various types of Typhonians has been stated in several places, but the details have now disappeared.[4] Though in the New

[1] *Hieratic Papyri in the British Museum* (Third Series), I, Text, pp. 10, 20, 21.

[2] In West Africa all children born with a red skin must be devoted to the service of the Thunder-god, P. A. Talbot, *Some Nigerian Fertility Cults*, p. 56. In mediaeval Europe there was a certain physical characteristic by which 'witches' were known, M. A. Murray, *The Witch-cult in Western Europe*, pp. 90–6. The European mark was quite different from the Egyptian.

[3] Red was evil, and therefore no doubt Seth's colour, at least as early as the Ebers Papyrus—of Hyksos date, Sethe, *Beiträge zur ältesten. Geschichte Ägyptens*, p. 127 (published in *Untersuchungen*, III).

[4] Fertility-rites everywhere become degraded into gross immorality. Seth was a god of this religion, and his immorality was famous. It is shown here as being intensified by drunkenness, which induced quarrelsomeness. By the Nineteenth Dynasty the decent Egyptians were too sophisticated to endure this gladly, just as were decent people in Europe in the seventeenth to the nineteenth centuries. Apart from the latter's dislike of a heathen religion their disapproval of the 'witches' of the old fertility-religion was for exactly the same reasons.

Kingdom at the Festivals of Hoeing the Earth the Seth-sacrifices clearly had their heads cut off, it is equally clear that on other occasions the sacrifice had been by fire. Thus, tradition recorded the death by fire of one Pharaoh who was Sethian in colouring. This was Nitocris, who was of a 'golden colour and with red cheeks', who 'cast herself into a room full of ashes' (p. 41). She is by no means the only Pharaoh who is said to have perished in, or escaped from, the flames, as will be seen in the course of this study. It is clear, therefore, that the official, historical, and religious records of Egypt do not ignore the duties of the divine king, who acted instead of the storm-god, controlled the weather, and supervised the fertility of the land and the health of the people. The folk-tales give them great pro-minence, and it is the popular ideas of Egypt which the classical writers have preserved to us.[1]

The memory and occasional practice of this custom of putting to death Seth and the king, or their substitutes, are very prominent in the classical authors, who provide further details. Thus, Plutarch says that the sacred animals in whom Typhon-Seth was incarnate were held accountable for the health of the people and a proper supply of water for their crops. If they failed in this duty 'excessive drought happens attended with pestilential diseases'. The priests then tried to frighten them back to good behaviour, and if that had no effect they put them to death. Whether this was done as a punishment, or as the supreme sacrifice, Plutarch was

The selfsame reasons still set the sheykhs against those relics of such practices as survive in modern Egypt. Yet again it was the licentious-ness of the Oriental religions that so scandalized Roman sobriety, and produced the fulminations of the early Christian Fathers. Cf. p. 102 *infra*

[1] Spiegelberg, *The Credibility of Herodotus' Account of Egypt in the Light of the Egyptian Monuments, passim*, especially pp. 31, 32.

unable to say.[1] As he records it, it was an occasional event, hence a punishment, which, however, took the form of the sacrifice, as in the case of the adulteresses to be studied later (pp. 54–57). It looks as if the same thing had been tried on a seventh century king of Ethiopia, who, however, proved strong enough to resist it (p. 63). Incorrigible guardians of the public welfare are liable to such punishment at the hands of their exasperated devotees. Thus, in Uganda and Kenya the Lango burned their rainmaker to death about one hundred years ago for failing to produce rain,[2] and in 1890 the Nandi clubbed theirs to death for allowing famine, sickness, and disastrous defeat to afflict them.[3] Similarly, in the middle of last century the Bari of the White Nile executed their rainmaker as being responsible for a four years' famine and other national disasters.[4] They also drove out his family and cattle.

After telling of the occasional treatment of the sacred animals, Plutarch goes on to record a similar, but different, story. He says: 'For truly, as Manetho has recorded, they used to burn living men to ashes in Eileithyiapolis, calling them Typhonians, and they used to scatter and dispose of their ashes by winnowing.'[5] Diodorus, I, 88, also states that anciently (τὸ παλαιόν) men of the colour of Typhon were sacrificed, but of this more later (p. 53). Plutarch's information supplements that given by the Pyramid Texts just quoted. The custom was evidently extremely ancient, for he says the sacrifice took place at the city of Eileithyia, that is to say at Nekheb-el Kab, the home of Nekhebt the

---

[1] *De Iside et Osiride*, § 73.
[2] Seligman, *Pagan Tribes*, p. 357.
[3] Hollis, *The Nandi*, pp. 49 ff. Other similar cases are quoted by Seligman, *Egypt and Negro Africa*, p. 6, note 1, p. 25.
[4] Seligman in *JRAI*, LVIII, p. 476.   [5] *Ibid.*

southern patroness of the king. Nekheb made a pair with Nekhen, Hierakonpolis, the prehistoric capital of southern Egypt, and it is here that the great place of burning was found (p. 53), and the scene depicting the Archaic king hoeing the ground (p. 19). Plutarch's information about the ashes is invaluable. It clinches the whole argument, for the scattering of ashes in the air is a well-known rain-charm and charm for promoting the fertility of the fields.[1]

Ammianus Marcellinus, XXVIII, 15, 14, quotes Egypt as a well-known example of the deposition of the king in case of military misfortunes or failure of the crops. A very famous character in classical literature was Busiris, a mythical king of Egypt.[2] The story went that after a nine years' drought a stranger from Cyprus predicted that the yearly sacrifice of a foreign man to Zeus would prevent such disasters.[3] Whereupon Busiris made him the first sacrifice, and continued so to sacrifice until he made the attempt upon Hercules who was passing through Egypt on his way from Libya. Hercules, however, turned the tables and sacrificed

---

[1] In mediaeval Europe the Devil (the heathen god incarnate) burned himself to ashes, and these were 'strown to awaken storm and tempest', and if the ashes of a 'witch' were 'scattered in the air, it should breed clouds, drought and hail', Grimm, *Teutonic Mythology* (trans. Stallybrass), p. 1087, cf. p. 1071. In America, on the Orinoco, the ashes of a human being are scattered to the winds under the belief that they are changed to rain, as are those of certain pieces of wood in New Granada, Frazer, *The Magic Art*, I, pp. 287, 304. In the same way the ashes of the human sacrifice are scattered over the fields as a fertilizer of magic potency by a Bechuana tribe in South Africa, and by the Khonds in India, id. *Spirits of the Corn and of the Wild*, I, pp. 240, 249. In modern Europe the ashes of what were once sacred fires are still scattered for the same purpose, id. *Balder the Beautiful*, pp. 141, 170, 190, 203, 250.

[2] Frazer has a great collection of passages referring to him in his editions of Apollodorus, *Bibliotheca*, I, p. 225.

[3] E.g. Apollodorus, *op. cit.* II, 5, 11; Ovid, *Ars Amatoria*, I, 647-52.

the king instead at the very altar used for the sacrifice of the foreigners.[1]

The story records the sacrifice of foreigners; that an attempt was made upon Hercules, who was a sky-god who was sacrificed; that Hercules reached Egypt from Libya; that Busiris tried to sacrifice this foreigner; but that Hercules sacrificed the king instead; that the sacrifice was to Zeus, i.e. the sky-god Amûn; finally, that this was one of the results of a nine years' drought.

The nine-year period is significant, for it occurs again in Egypt, and is well known in the sky-fertility-religions of other lands.[2] Hercules figures in Manetho as the name of Osorcho or Osorthon, who is said to have reigned for nine years (Eusebius),[3] or possibly only eight (Africanus).[4] Hercules entered Egypt from Libya, and the time of the Osorkons was one of strong Libyan influence in Egypt, and the beginning of closer Egyptian intercourse with the Libyan oases.[5] The city of Hercules, Heracle-

[1] Pherecydes in Didot, *Fragm. Hist. Graec.* I, pp. 78, 79, Fragment 33.

[2] See pp. 78–80 *infra*.

[3] In all the chaos of copyists it is clear that what Eusebius had copied from Manetho was 'Osorthon, 9 years, whom the Egyptians called Hercules', for all Eusebius' copyists agree here. Eusebius copied Manetho in the early fourth century A.D., but his book is lost and is now only known in the following works; the fifth century A.D. Armenian translation, Aucher, I, p. 218; II, p. 169; Jerome's late fourth century A.D. Latin translation of the latter part of the book, Schoene, II (*Can*), p. 75; the eighth century A.D. extract in Georgius Syncellus, *Chronographia*, Dindorf, p. 140. Worse still the manuscripts on which we have to work today are not the original books of the copyists whose names they bear, but copies again by later hands.

[4] Africanus copied Manetho in the early third century A.D., but his work is also lost and is now only known in the eighth century extract in Georgius Syncellus, *op. cit.* p. 138. It reads 'Osorcho, 8 years, whom the Egyptians call Hercules'.

[5] For the Libyan influences at this time in Egypt, see Wainwright in *Anns. Serv.* XXVII, pp. 103, 104; B. *A.R.* IV, §§ 815, 830, 873, where

opolis, was one of the places where the earth was ceremonially hoed with blood (p. 30) and it had been very
prominent under the Twenty-Second Dynasty, which was
Libyan. The descendants of Buyuwawa the Libyan held a
priesthood there for five generations, and finally one of them
became 'High priest of Heracleopolis, Commander of the
army'.[1] The priests of Heracleopolis were as much a power
in the land as were the high priests of Amûn at Thebes, or
the chiefs of the Meshwesh (Libyans),[2] and the commander
at that city was one of the leading men in Egypt.[3] The city
also played a leading part in the wars with Piankhi, though
on the Ethiopian, not the Egyptian, side. The classical story
is one of struggle with varying success, which is what this
period was in actual fact. The Ethiopians under Piankhi
held a good deal of the country, the Egyptians, mostly under
Libyan leaders, revolted from them, were conquered, and
afterwards took control of their own land once more.
Tefnakhte, who led the revolt, was described as 'Chief of the
West'[4] or as 'Chief of Me (Meshwesh, Libyans)',[5] and of
the three contemporary kinglets who wore the royal uraeus
one was the king of Heracleopolis, and another was
Osorkon III.[6] After Piankhi's conquest of Egypt and return

various kinglets wear the Libyan feather; Breasted, *A History of Egypt*,
pp. 526 ff. For Egyptian influence in the Oases, see B. *A.R.* IV, §§734,
782, 784; Gardiner in *JEA*, XIX, pp. 21, 22; Steindorff in *ZÄS*, LXIX,
pp. 21, 23.

[1] B. *A.R.* IV, § 787, no. 11.
[2] B. *A.R.* IV, § 747. The Chiefs of the Meshwesh, generally con-
tracted into Me (B. *A.R.* IV, § 779, note c), were everywhere in the
country (B. *A.R.* V, *Index*, p. 53) and the grandson of one of them
became king of Egypt as Sheshonk I (B. *A.R.* IV, § 669, note e).
[3] Id. *op. cit.* § 777.   [4] Id. *op. cit.* § 818.
[5] Id. *op. cit.* §§ 838, 854, 880. In § 822 Piankhi specifies Libyans,
Ṯḥnw, as Tefnakhte's main support.
[6] Id. *op. cit.* § 814, and cf. § 852.

to Ethiopia, Osorkon III regained control of Thebes,[1] and Tefnakhte was father of Bocchoris,[2] the king whose sacrifice by an Ethiopian will be discussed shortly. In the actual historical account religion is prominent, for all through Piankhi emphasizes his own orthodoxy and care for religion, and the uncleanness of his opponents. The Ethiopian kings were themselves of Libyan extraction. Their ancestors had only reached Napata less than two hundred years before, where they lived in their primitive barbarism for at least the first two generations.[3] About the time of their arrival the hierarchy of the Theban god, which had long had a strong hold on the country, had strengthened this hold into full possession.[4] Hence, the first steps of the Ethiopian dynasty towards civilization had been taken under the guidance of the priests of Amûn, who clearly found in them devoted adherents. Amûn belonged to the Egyptian sky-fertility-religion, which was only a civilized form of Libyan barbarism. Hence, the Libyo-Ethiopians countenanced no relaxation of ancient custom, but exacted the full measure of the law. In its legendary form the struggle is entirely religious, concerning a drought, a period of nine years, and the sacrifice of a king, to prevent the recurrence of the disaster. Such kings are the incarnation of the god, and the story also concerns the attempted sacrifice of Hercules, and it was Hercules who eventually sacrificed the king. Hercules not only represented a definite king of Egypt at the time of the Ethiopian encroachment as has just been seen, but was

---

[1] Id. *op. cit.* §§ 811, and 872, note d.

[2] Mentioned in recognizable versions in several of the classical authors, e.g. Diod. I, 45; Plut. *De Iside et Osiride*, § 8.

[3] Reisner in *Museum of Fine Arts Bulletin* (Boston, 1921), XIX, pp. 26, 28.

[4] Breasted, *A History of Egypt*, pp. 538, 539; cf. Reisner in *JEA*, VI, pp. 54, 55.

also a storm-god who sacrificed himself by fire (pp. 6, 49, 64 note 1), and as Strabo (xvii, 2, § 3) and Diodorus (iii, 9) show, his name was given by the Greeks to the Ethiopian Amûn.[1]

Thus, like so many other classical stories of Egypt, that of Busiris and Hercules is folk-lore. It refers to the eighth century B.C. and to the struggles of the Libyans, whether masquerading as Egyptians or Ethiopians. Further, it is the religious history of these struggles that it preserves, and of this it perpetuates the essentials with considerable accuracy. It should be noted that both in fact and in story Libya is once more prominent as so often before.

Bocchoris was another Pharaoh, and his life and fate made only less impression on the classical world than those of Busiris. The stories about Bocchoris were legion,[2] but only those which deal with his fate can be discussed here. They show clearly that what came to him was the ancient penalty of kingship under the Old Religion.

Africanus records that Bocchoris reigned six years,[3] and this seems to be a genuine piece of history, for we possess three records of his reign referring to an event in his sixth year and nothing later.[4] Diodorus, i, 65, reports that Bocchoris 'in sagacity much excelled the former kings'. Elsewhere, i, 94, in recording the lawgivers of Egypt he says that Bocchoris was 'a wise sort of man and conspicuous for his craftiness' and that 'he set in order all things concerning the kings', and he is the only one of whom Diodorus says anything of the sort. Josephus says that in consequence of pestilence and

---

[1] Herodotus, ii, 42, brings them together in a curious passage recording a visit of Hercules to the Theban Amûn.

[2] Moret has studied a large collection of them in his *De Bocchori Rege*.

[3] Dindorf, p. 138. For the other years ascribed to him, forty-six and forty-four, see p. 46 note 3 *infra*.

[4] B. *A.R.* iv, § 884.

dearth Bocchoris 'sent to enquire of the oracle of Ammon respecting the unfruitfulness (περὶ τῆς ἀκαρπίας)'. The reply instructed him to expel the diseased, and to purify the temples, 'and thus the land would produce fruit (καρπο-φορήσειν)'.[1] Manetho records that 'a lamb spoke'[2] in the reign of Bocchoris and that the Pharaoh 'was burned alive',[3] the lamb of course being Amûn, one of the gods of that sky-religion which demands the sacrifice of the king. This wise and prudent Bocchoris met his death at the hands of Sabacon, his successor. Yet, instead of being considered a ruthless murderer, Sabacon has gone down in legend as obedient to the gods and unwilling to offend them (Hdt. II, 139), of reasonable disposition (ἐπιεικείας), opposed to capital punishment, and as having 'much excelled his predecessors in piety and uprightness' (Diod. I, 65). Herodotus, II, 137, 140, calls Sabacon's victim Anysis, and says he escaped to the Delta, whence he finally emerged from the 'ashes and earth' which had been collected around him. Here we seem to hear of an escape from the fire, such as is recorded later on of Sesostris and of the mummy of Amasis, and is a common amelioration of the penalty of such kingships.

This catalogue of events makes it pretty clear what happened. Nature had failed to function, and famine and epidemics had ensued. The sky-god Amûn was consulted, when it transpired that the practice of that religion which affected this sort of thing had grown slack. Bocchoris was

---

[1] Josephus, *Contra Apionem*, I, 306, who gives it as the cause of the Exodus.

[2] In all the copies of Eusebius' extracts from Manetho, Aucher, I, p. 218; II, p. 171; Schoene, II, p. 77; Dindorf, p. 140. Also in Africanus' extract of Manetho, Dindorf, p. 138.

[3] Eusebius in Aucher, I, p. 218; II, p. 177; Schoene, II, p. 83; Dindorf, p. 140. Africanus in Dindorf, p. 138.

of Libyan extraction (p. 37), lived at a time of strong Libyan influence in Egypt, and was put to death by a semi-barbarous worshipper of Amûn, also of Libyan extraction. Also Bocchoris was wise, and his wisdom consisted in setting in order everything concerned with the kingship. This clearly resulted in his undertaking the sacrifice which the primitive sky-fertility-religion demanded of the king in such circumstances.[1] In actuality he does not seem to have undertaken the sacrifice so much as to have had it thrust upon him by an ardent upholder of the ancient law in all its rigour. It was evidently as a result of this that he acquired what seems to be a nickname Ἄννσις, 'Completion', as having completed the supreme duty of a divine king in laying down his life for his people. Moreover, Bocchoris-Anysis met his death at the hands of his successor; another characteristic of the divine king who controls the weather, and one which will be met shortly in Sesostris under similar conditions. Further, this successor, Sabacon, was also of Libyan origin, and was king of Ethiopia where Amûn, the sky-god, held absolute sway, and where kings were still to be put to death by the priests for another five hundred years (p. 52). It may be that the apocryphal eight years which Africanus gives to Sabacon[2] may represent a supposed lease of life of seven years, at the end of which he in his turn met his own death. The fact that instead of being considered a criminal, Sabacon acquired the reputation of

---

[1] The story of his reputed 'judgment of Solomon' (Moret, *De Bocchori Rege*, pp. 57–61) might have accrued to him through his fame for wisdom, though actually his wisdom concerned something very different.

[2] Dindorf, p. 138. The historical king Shabaka reigned at least twelve years (B. *A.R.* IV, p. 451), which is the number given to Sabacon in Eusebius' quotation from Manetho, Aucher, I, p. 218; II, p. 177; Schoene, II, p. 83; Dindorf, p. 140.

extreme care in the worship of the gods suggests that his procedure was in some way correct.

Both of the stories of Busiris and Bocchoris refer to the same period, that of the Twenty-Second to the Twenty-Fifth Dynasties. It was a time of encroachment by Libya upon Egypt. This encroachment came from two directions; directly from the west in the persons of Hercules and of Bocchoris through his father Tefnakhte; and indirectly from the south in the persons of Piankhi and Sabacon, for by origin the Ethiopians were southern Libyans. Both brought the ancient custom of sacrificing the king, and carried out on the more civilized soil of Egypt the age-old barbarities of the more primitive Libya. In Egypt the kings had long ago been able to commute their fate, but in Libya the old law clearly held sway, as it still continued to do in Ethiopia for long afterwards. It was the horror of such savageries that found them a place, whether in the official histories such as Manetho's, or in the folk-lore stories of old times.

Nitocris was another Pharaoh of whom there was a story of a six-year reign ending in ashes. Moreover, there is good evidence that she was divine, had to do with fertility, and brought her people the victory expected of such rulers. Herodotus says (II, 100) that the Egyptians slew their king and gave the kingdom to his sister Nitocris. She drowned his murderers, and 'cast herself into a room full of ashes', committing suicide thereby. The reign of six years comes from an independent, but very strange, list of kings compiled by Eratosthenes and preserved by Syncellus.[1] Other

---

[1] Dindorf, p. 195. Africanus gives twelve years, Dindorf, p. 108. Eusebius omits any length for her reign. Her supposed 203 years which gives rise to the three years (Dindorf, p. 109) is really the total for the dynasty, cf. Africanus (Dindorf, p. 108) and Eusebius himself elsewhere (Aucher, I, p. 209).

writers give further clues. In the Armenian translation of his book Eusebius, copying from Manetho, says that Nitocris was of a 'golden colour and with red cheeks', or as the modern editor has Latinized it 'flavo colore, et rubris genis'.[1] This passage is reproduced by Syncellus, who says that she was most beautiful, 'having the advantage of a fair (ξανθή) complexion',[2] and Africanus uses the same word.[3] The tradition of her redness was apparently very strong, for while these two authors say it was she who built the Third Pyramid, others say it was Rhodopis.[4] Now, Rhodopis means 'rosy-cheeked'.

This strong tradition of a golden-coloured queen of the Old Kingdom records a fact. A contemporary tomb has been found which shows pictures of Ḥetep-ḥeres II, the daughter of Khufu and queen of one of his successors. These paintings show her with the usual long black wig of the period, and once with short hair which would be her own. While the short hair of the other ladies is black as usual, the queen's is almost unique in being carefully 'painted a bright yellow with fine red horizontal lines'.[5] In the Fifth Dynasty there is another lady who is named Ḥetep-ḥeres, and she may be the granddaughter of the other. Her hair also is painted yellow.[6] Thus, the epithet of a 'golden colour' which Eusebius says Manetho gave to Nitocris exactly describes the colour of the hair of at least two ladies of the Old Kingdom, one of whom was a queen. Classical tradition, therefore, contains a kernel of

---

[1] Aucher, I, p. 209.

[2] Dindorf, p. 109, ξανθή τε τὴν χροιὰν ὑπάρξασα.

[3] Id. *op. cit.* p. 108.

[4] Diod. I, 64; Strabo, xvII, i, 33; Pliny, *Nat. Hist.* xxxvi, 12 (17).

[5] Reisner in *Museum of Fine Arts Bulletin* (Boston, 1927), xxv, p. 66 and figs. 5, 7. Unfortunately her royal husband is not named.

[6] L. *D.* II, Pl. 90; Scharff in *OLZ*, 1928, col. 80.

truth when it ascribes the Third Pyramid either to the golden-coloured queen Nitocris, or to the 'rosy-cheeked' courtesan Rhodopis. Yet another confirmation of the general accuracy of tradition lies in the fact that the name of the queen is given as Nitocris (Egyptian, Neithaqert), which alludes to the goddess Neith. This appears in the fact that about the time of the building of the Third Pyramid two priestesses of Neith bore the same name as the queen. One of them at least was fair-headed and was probably a granddaughter of the queen Ḥetep-ḥeres, as mentioned above.[1]

As there prove to be so many scraps of truth embedded in the classical story, there may also be a germ of truth in the details concerning Nitocris' divinity, her fertility aspect, her reign of six years, her fiery death, and her probable connexion with Libya to be seen in the next paragraph.

The details of the Nitocris story and the characteristics of the Ḥetep-ḥeres ladies, upon whom it is founded, carry our argument yet another step further. They introduce Libya once more. Both the Nitocris of story and two of the Ḥetep-ḥeres ladies of fact were fair, a peculiarity for which certain Libyans were famous. In a well-known picture of the Twelfth Dynasty the Libyan woman has a white skin and red hair and, in the present condition of the painting, blue eyes, as has her child.[2] The man also has red hair, and

---

[1] L. D. II, Pl. 90; Mariette, *Mastabas*, p. 90, B, 2; Scharff, *op. cit.* col. 81. They belong to the early Fifth Dynasty.

[2] Newberry, *Beni Hasan*, I, Pl. xlv. These unnamed foreigners have always been accepted as Libyans, and now Möller in *ZDMG*, LXXVIII (1924), p. 45, note 1, points out that quite similar figures are labelled Temehu (southern Libyans) by Hatshepsut, Naville, *Deir el Bahari*, Pl. xc, end of the bottom register. The question as to the colour of the eyes arises from the fact that the paintings are very rubbed here, and when the 'black' used by the Egyptians rubs off, it regularly

a skin fairer than the usual Egyptian, though it is not so light as the woman's. As of Nitocris, so of the Libyans, the classical authors regularly use the word ξανθός,[1] and a voyager of the fourteenth century says of the Berber-speaking aborigines of the Canary Islands 'crines habent longos et flavos'.[2] 'Flavus' is the modern editor's Latin for the Armenian word applied to Nitocris.[3] Nitocris' colouring was also that of Seth, and again he was important in Libya (p. 13). To the question of colouring must be added the connexions with Neith which have just been enumerated. They point in the same direction, for Neith was the great goddess of the western Delta on the confines of Libya.

Whether Libyan or not, in having a fair or red complexion Nitocris was clearly one of the red Typhonians who were sacrificed by fire (pp. 33, 53) for the welfare of the people.

leaves a blue patch. This, however, may not come into consideration here, as the well-known Libyan in the tomb of Ramosy has grey eyes, as has the Syrian, in opposition to the two negroes who have black ones, Prisse d'Avennes, *Histoire de l'art égyptien*, II, *Dessin*, Pl. iv, and Pausanias, I, 14, 6, speaks of 'grey eyes' (γλαυκούς...ὀφθαλμούς) as being characteristic of the Libyans. Cf. p. 102 *infra*.

[1] Callimachus, *Hymn*, II, l. 85; Scylax, *Periplus*, § 110 (C. Müller, *Geogr. Graec. Min.* I, p. 88); Procopius, *De Bello Vandalico*, II, 13, 29. See Bates, *The Eastern Libyans*, p. 40. He, however, and following him Möller in *op. cit.* pp. 46, 47, are in error in supposing that Lucan applies 'flavus' and 'rutilus' to the Libyans. Actually the words are used of others in opposition to the Libyans.

[2] Möller in *op. cit.* p. 58.

[3] Though hardly likely in view of the above evidence for Libya, the possibility should not be overlooked that red-headed foreigners might have come from the north. The Kurds have 'generally blue eyes and fair hair' (von Luschan in *JRAI*, 1911, p. 229), and among the Druzes of Bashan 'blue eyes and brown hair are common' (E. Huntington, *Palestine and its Transformation*, p. 244). There is a fair, red-haired type of Jew known as the 'pseudo-Gentile' (R. N. Salaman in *Journal of Genetics*, I (1911), p. 288), and David himself is described as being 'ruddy' (1 Sam. xvi, 12; xvii, 42). Such red-headed men may be met in Egypt today in Cairo and the Eastern Delta.

Her self-immolation in the fire is a genuine Egyptian conception. For in the Twelfth Dynasty the Man Weary of Life speaks of the time 'when I strive for death before it has come to me, and when I cast myself into the fire in order to burn myself up'.[1] The fertility theme is introduced by the story of her under the name of Rhodopis, for she was said to be a courtesan.[2] Finally, Eratosthenes' remark (*loc. cit.*), that 'she is Athene Nicephorus', i.e. a divinity who brings victory, suggests that her death by fire was a sacrifice or an apotheosis.[3] Thus, Nitocris is called 'The Victory Bringer' just as in the Nineteenth Dynasty Ramesses II was acclaimed by his courtiers as 'Greatly victorious; He whose terror hath crushed foreign lands' and much else in the same strain (p. 17). It may be worth mentioning that shortly after the end of the Sixth Dynasty, when she lived, Heracleopolis came to the fore, as the place of origin of the Ninth and Tenth Dynasties. This was the city that was prominent in the Libyan period of the Twenty-Second to the Twenty-Fourth Dynasties. The last of these kings was Bocchoris who, like Nitocris, perished in the fire after a reign of six years (pp. 38, 39). Heracleopolis was also one of the places where the ceremony of hoeing the earth with blood was carried out (p. 30).

As in the stories of Bocchoris and Nitocris, a period of six

---

[1] Scharff, *Der Bericht über das Streitgespräch eines Lebensmüden mit seiner Seele*, p. 12, l. 13 (published in *Sitzungsb. der Bay. Ak. der Wiss. Phil.-hist. Abt.*, 1937, Heft 9). On p. 15 note 15 Scharff remarks that this passage is one of the unintelligible things of which Egyptian religion is full. The present study will perhaps help to clear up the difficulty.

[2] Hdt. II, 134; Diod. I, 64; Pliny, *Nat. Hist.* XXXVI, 12 (17). Strabo, XVII, 1, 33, knows the story, but thinks she was the wife of one of the Pharaohs, as does Aelian, *Var. Hist.* XIII, 33.

[3] Maspero supposes that 'Athene Nicephorus' is merely a bad translation of Neithaqert, *Rec. de Trav.* 1895, pp. 73, 74. There is more in it, however, than that.

years enters into the strange tale of Mycerinus. This was not his only resemblance to Bocchoris, for of him also legend said that he 'made the most righteous judgments of all their kings' and was religious.[1] He permitted the Egyptians 'to return to sacrifices' (Hdt. II, 129). Yet this religious king was condemned to an early death by the gods whom he served (id. ii, 133). There is a further similarity between the stories of the two kings and the practices of the sky-fertility-religion. It is that both of them met their death in their seventh year. The oracle told Mycerinus 'that he had no more than six years to live, and should die in the seventh' (id. II, 133). As it is recorded of Bocchoris that he reigned six years,[2] it is to be supposed that he also died in his seventh year. This seems to be a genuine piece of history, for his sixth year is the highest known from his monuments.[3] Similarly, if Nitocris reigned six years she presumably died in her seventh year. In countries other than Egypt seven

[1] Petrie, *History* (10th ed.), I, 117, gives a brilliant explanation as to how a Sixth Dynasty queen became connected with the Third Pyramid. This was built by Men-kau-rê in the Fourth Dynasty, and at the end of the Sixth Dynasty the Abydos list gives a name Men-ka-rê, but the Turin Papyrus gives a name Neithaqert. Nitocris is clearly Neithaqert, and Neithaqert no doubt is Men-ka-rê. This name the classical writers no doubt confused with Men-kau-rê, the real builder of the Third Pyramid. Möller in *ƵÄS*, LVI, pp. 76, 77, thinks that Herodotus confused the names of the two kings *Bk-n-rn-f* and Men-kau-rê and explains his misplacing of the Fourth Dynasty in this way. A better derivation for the form Bocchoris seems to be that advanced by Breasted, *A.R.* IV, p. 447, note c. He would find it not in the personal name, Bk-n-rn-f, but in the throne name Wahkarê (*w3ḥ-k3-rᶜ*).   [2] Africanus in Dindorf, p. 138.

[3] Petrie, *History*, III, pp. 316, 317. If Eusebius happens to have preserved the right length of reign for Sabacon, he has gone very wrong over Bocchoris. Both entries in the Armenian translation give him forty-four years (Aucher, I, p. 218; II, p. 171), as does Syncellus' copy (Dindorf, p. 140). Forty-four is no doubt a dittography, for the number occurs several times in this neighbourhood, and Jerome's forty-six (Schoene, II, p. 77) is no doubt a further mistake.

Plate I

NEUSERRÊ RECEIVING SEVEN LIVES FROM ANUBIS THE DEATH-GOD

years is a well-known 'span of life' granted to victims of the Old Religion.[1] As Dr Margaret Murray points out, there is undoubtedly substance in the tale of Mycerinus, for she has just published a scene where another Old Kingdom Pharaoh, Neuserrê, is supported by the goddess Wazet-Buto, while the death-god, Anubis, presents him with seven lives, *ankhs*, Pl. I.[2] As so often, here again Libya appears, for the Nile-gods supporting the throne do not wear their usual boatman's girdle, but the penistasche, the standard dress of Libya all through Pharaonic days.

A story of some detail was current in Greek times, portions of which have been preserved by Herodotus (II, 107), Diodorus Siculus (I, 55, 57), Josephus (*Contra Apionem*, I, §§ 98–101), and Eusebius (Aucher, I, pp. 211, 232–4; Dindorf, pp. 111, 112). It concerns a king called Sesostris by Herodotus and by Eusebius in one place (Aucher, p. 211; Dindorf, pp. 111, 112), Sesoosis by Diodorus, and 'Sethos who is also Ramesses' by Josephus and by Eusebius in another place (Aucher, pp. 232, 233). What interests us here is that the king had been away on his conquests a good long time (Jos., Eus. (p. 233)), or more precisely nine years (Diod., Eus. (pp. 211, 111, 112)),[3] when 'He who was

---

[1] M. A. Murray, *The God of the Witches*, pp. 134, 135, 158, 159.

[2] Id. in *Mélanges Maspero*, I, pp. 252, 253 and fig. 2 (*Méms. de l'Inst. fr. du Caire*, LXVI) = Borchardt, *Das Grabdenkmal des Königs Ne-user-re^c*, Blatt 16.

[3] Eusebius preserves most of the details of the conquests, and all versions of him preserve the nine years. He gives the story as an extract from Manetho. Unfortunately he breaks it up into two parts; the conquests with the name Sesostris which he transfers to the Twelfth Dynasty, and the return to Egypt which he gives much later under the name 'Sethos who is also Ramesses'. The nine years occur again in an extract which is probably from Africanus. He is the other copyist of Manetho, extracts from whom Syncellus intercalates with the parallel passage from Eusebius. Unfortunately Syncellus has marked these two parallel passages as both being from Eusebius.

appointed over the sacrifices of Egypt' (Jos.,[1] Eus. (p. 233))
informed him that a new king had arisen. It was his brother
whom he had left as regent (Hdt., Jos.), who had possessed
the queen by force, was continually using the royal concubines, and was wearing the crown (Jos., Eus. (p. 233)).
At Pelusian Daphnae (Hdt.) or at Pelusium itself (Diod.,
Jos., Eus. (p. 233)), Sesostris' brother feasted him, his wife,
and sons, and then set fire to the house or tent (Hdt., Diod.).
Sesostris got little or no help from his retinue, for they were
'like drunken men' (Diod.), but he escaped through the
flames (Hdt., Diod.). Though Diodorus implies that the
wife and sons all perished, Herodotus states that two of his
sons laid down their lives to facilitate the escape of their
father and the others.

The essence of this story is that after a period of nine years
an attempt was made to burn the old king to death by the
man who had made himself the successor. Its basic truth
appears in many details, which conform to the pattern of
a rainmaker's life and death. Such details are that the
attempt was made on the king after a period of nine years,
a custom well known in fertility-rites; that he was to have
met his end by fire[2] as the divine victim often does; that he

---

[1] ὁ τεταγμένος ἐπὶ τῶν ἱερῶν τῆς Αἰγύπτου. ἱερῶν of course might
merely mean 'temples' as the Armenian translator of Eusebius' copy
of this story has prudently rendered it, Aucher, I, p. 233, but see
Aucher's note 3. Cf. pp. 102-6 infra.

[2] The clumsy expedient of burning down the house is not so fantastic
as it might appear. A famine once arose in Sweden, which people
ascribed to the lack of sacrifices by the king. They, therefore, 'sur-
rounded his house, and burnt him in it, giving him to Odin as a
sacrifice for good crops', S. Laing, The Heimskringla (London, 1889),
I, p. 323. Apart from the question of sacrifice the story of another
ancient king of Sweden is even more closely parallel to that of Sesostris.
That king is said to have destroyed his rivals by setting fire to the hall
in which he had feasted them and made them all drunk, id. op. cit.
I, p. 316. This story was repeated in actual fact at Shendy in the Sudan

escaped, as the victim is often allowed to do; that others perished on his behalf, as is often the case; that the attempt was made by one of the royal family; that this man had married the royal women and was the successor; and that the king's guards made little or no attempt to save him.

The parallels offered by the modern Sudan have already been mentioned, p. 5, where the Fung king has regularly been slain by his successor, who must be of the royal lineage, as is also the case among the Shilluks.[1] The Shilluk parallel goes further, for it is a point of honour with the king not to call upon his guards for help at this crisis.[2] In the story of Sesostris his successor tried to put him to death by fire, just as Sabacon sacrificed Bocchoris, and as Cambyses wished to treat the mummy of Amasis. The taking of the victim's women by the slayer appears again in the fertility-rites. In arranging his own death by fire Hercules instructed his eldest son, Hyllus, to burn him to death on the pyre without tears or lamentation and to succeed in marriage to Iole, his favourite concubine.[3] At the Sacaea festival in Babylon a Mock King replaced the real king for the occasion, after which he died the death. During his few days' reign he enjoyed the royal concubines.[4] The death of Sesostris' sons

in 1822. The natives there destroyed Ismail Pasha and the officers of his invading army by setting fire to the house where they were sleeping off the effects of a feast, Cailliaud, *Voyage à Méroé*, III, pp. 336, 337. Sardanapalus was said to have set fire to his own palace, destroying himself, his women, his household, and his goods in the flames rather than fall into the enemies' hands, Diodorus, II, 27.

[1] Elsewhere the king was killed by the high officer of the court whose duty this was, Seligman, *Pagan Tribes*, p. 423.

[2] Id. *op. cit.* p. 91.

[3] Sophocles, *Trachiniae*, ll. 1195–201, 1220–6.

[4] Frazer, *The Dying God*, p. 114. To take the royal women is to become king. When Absalom drove out David he 'went in unto his father's concubines', II Sam. xvi, 22. When Adonijah asked for one of the previous king's women, Abishag, in marriage, Solomon replied

and the nine-year period both find their counterpart in the legend of the king of Sweden who for nine periods of nine years each used to sacrifice one of his sons to secure his own lease of life.[1] Nine of course is very common in this connexion, and has already been met in the Busiris story (p. 34 *supra*). Hence the sacrifice of Sesostris' sons is an integral part of the story.[2] Elsewhere Diodorus (I, 58) also records that Sesoosis, as he calls him, committed suicide, 'for which he was admired not only by the priests, but by all the rest of the Egyptians'. Similarly Nitocris, who committed suicide in the fire, was or became a goddess (p. 45 *supra*). Clearly, therefore, there was something religious and sacrificial about the death of a Pharaoh. Spiegelberg has already pointed out that Cleopatra gained apotheosis through suicide.[3]

It is evident, therefore, that the Pharaohs were considered to be divine; to have power in the air. They took their part in agriculture. In other words they were, or had been, held responsible for the welfare of their people and their crops.[4]

'ask for him the kingdom also' and immediately had him murdered, I Kings ii, 22–25. For other cases see Frazer, *The Magic Art*, II, pp. 281–3; M. A. Murray in *JRAI*, XLV, pp. 307 ff.

[1] Frazer, *The Dying God*, pp. 160, 161.

[2] The details no doubt owed their form to local Egyptian conditions. Maspero shows convincingly how the wife and four sons got into the story, *La geste de Sésostris* in *Études de myth. et d'arch. ég.* VIII, pp. 8, 9, 16 (*Bibl. ég.* XL (1916)). The art motif of the king trampling on his enemies is invoked by Spiegelberg in *Klio*, XIX, pp. 101, 102, and *The Credibility of Herodotus' Account of Egypt in the Light of the Egyptian Monuments*, p. 25, to account for the story. Though this may account for Sesostris' stepping on the bodies, it is not the whole explanation.

[3] *Sitzungsb. der Bay. Ak. der Wiss., Philos.-philol.-hist. Klasse*, 1925, Nr. 2, pp. 3–6.

[4] As indeed Moret recognized long ago in his *Royauté dans l'Égypte primitive* (published in *Conférences faites au musée Guimet, Bibliothèque de Vulgarisation*, XXXVIII, 1912), pp. 215 ff.

It is also evident that like Seth, the storm-god, they were liable to a ceremonial death, and that like him that death was, or had been, by fire. That responsibility goes back to the remote period in Libya before the occupation of the Nile Valley, when the crops had been dependent on the rain, not on the inundation of the Nile. It is also evident that the custom of sacrificing the Pharaoh by fire fell early into desuetude, but that tales of this fate might reasonably be told of such a king as Ramesses II (Sesostris, Sesoosis, Sethos who is also Ramesses), who, as we know, definitely claimed power over the elements. It is also evident that a recrudescence of the primitive custom actually took place in the eighth century B.C. under influence from that Libya whence the idea originally reached Egypt.

Kings, or their substitutes, all the world over have undertaken their sacrifice gladly. In fact, in modern times, when for one reason or another their death would have been dangerous for their sacrificers, they have often earnestly begged to be allowed to die in the manner of their ancestors.[1] But still, in the course of time, others have rebelled against the destiny hanging over them. Increasing civilization and gradual advance in philosophy have shown how the rigour of the law may be tempered, as seen on pp. 4, 5.

Sometimes a human substitute is found for the king, and sometimes an animal is considered sufficient, or finally a vegetable or even an inanimate object.[2] At times the king

[1] Seligman, *Egypt and Negro Africa*, pp. 6, 21; id. *Pagan Tribes*, pp. 196, 197; Murray, *The Witch-cult in Western Europe*, pp. 160, 162; id. *The God of the Witches*, pp. 135, 136.

[2] The chief of one of the tribes of Uganda used to provide one of his sons as the sacrifice to invigorate the king, Roscoe, *The Baganda*, pp. 210, 211. In India a certain family holds its lands on condition that it provides the victim at the required time, Frazer, *The Dying God*, p. 56. In West Africa apes, considered by the natives to be degenerate men, are used as substitutes for the human sacrifice, or even anthills

[51]   4-2

enacts his own death. Sometimes the amelioration is due to the introduction of foreign and more advanced modes of thought. Thus, in the third century B.C. Ergamenes, king of Ethiopia, had been educated in the Greek way. Hence, when he received the summons to take his own life, instead of submitting he marched on the temple and slew the priests;[1] a story which was repeated in detail by the king of Eyeo in West Africa about A.D. 1774.[2] Similarly, two centuries ago the rainmaking king of Sofala in south-eastern Africa refused to commit suicide at the appointed time.[3]

In Egypt we already know that the divine Pharaoh did impersonate the gods, at least on some occasions.[4] We also know that in the ancient fertility ceremonies the king's fate had been that of Seth (pp. 26, 27), and several stories have been quoted of the sacrifice of the Pharaoh by fire. In the case of Sesostris we seem to hear of the sacrifice in the flames of substitutes, so that the king might escape his lawful fate.

dressed up for the occasion, P. A. Talbot, *In the Shadow of the Bush*, p. 78. In Europe today it is often an effigy that is burned, see p. 57 note 1, p. 58 *infra*. At Fazogli in the Sudan a dog is now killed in place of the king at the yearly festival, Seligman, *Pagan Tribes*, p. 425. The Indians of Natal lead a goat to the place of sacrifice, but there actually cut a pumpkin in two, instead of cutting the animal's throat, Sayce in *Man*, 1933, p. 6.

[1] Diodorus, III, 6, gives the name of the king and the fact of his Greek education, and mentions the subjection of the kings to the priests. Strabo, XVII, ii, 3, repeats the story, adding that the priests appointed the new king after the suicide of the old.

[2] Frazer, *The Dying God*, p. 41.

[3] Id. *op. cit.* p. 38.

[4] Dr Murray points out to me that Hatshepsut's father was Tethmosy I, yet her birth was 'miraculous', for she says that her 'bodily' father was Amûn, B. A.R. II, § 208. This could not have been unless Tethmosy I had impersonated the god, and in fact we are told in the crudest language how Amûn 'made his form like the majesty of this husband, the king Okheperkere (Thutmose I), etc., etc.', *op. cit.* §§ 196–8.

Plutarch says:[1] 'For truly, as Manetho has recorded, they used to burn living men to ashes in Eileithyiapolis, calling them Typhonians, and they used to scatter and dispose of their ashes by winnowing.' Diodorus is just as explicit, and adds another piece of information. He says, 1, 88, that 'anciently (τὸ παλαιόν) men who were similarly coloured to Typhon were sacrificed by the kings'. In being burned alive these men were put to death in the manner of certain Pharaohs, whether of Nitocris and Bocchoris, or of the attempt on Sesostris, and Nitocris we are told was red, hence Typhonian in complexion. Moreover, these men were sacrificed 'by the kings'. Thus, they were no doubt substitutes for the kings themselves, just as the kings had been the substitutes on earth for the god in heaven. It was not difficult to make the deduction that if the king could represent the god, some other man could represent the king. Though no place of burning has been reported from el Kab-Nekheb-Eileithyiapolis, one has been from Nekhen-Hierakonpolis just opposite across the river, and the site of a great Predynastic city and the ancient capital of Egypt.[2] In the centre of this Predynastic city a space of bare rock was covered with a thick crust of charred wood, bones, and other debris. It must have been of some size, for the pile of stones with which it was covered suggested a burial tumulus to the finders. Unfortunately no mention is made of the kind of bones which had been burned.

By the early Eighteenth Dynasty in some at least of the Seth-sacrifices animals had been substituted for men. At the Festival of Hoeing the Ground it is said that 'the Companions of Seth came, and changed themselves into goats',

---

[1] *De Iside et Osiride*, § 73.

[2] Lansing in *Bull. Metrop. Mus. of Art* (New York), Nov. 1935: *The Egyptian Expedition*, 1934–5, p. 44.

when they were slaughtered.[1] This step is also reflected in the classical authors. Diodorus, I, 88, says that still in his time 'Red oxen, however, may be sacrificed, because it is thought that this was the colour of Typhon', just as Plutarch says that animals sacred to Typhon-Seth were sacrificed, at least on occasion (p. 32). Diodorus had good authority for his statement, and like the ancient Seth-sacrifices of men that of the red goat and the red ox was by fire. For the Festival Calendar at Edfu says: 'Let a red goat and a red ox be brought; let his intestines be taken out; let a great burnt sacrifice be made, whilst his belly is filled with all sweet-scented spices.'[2] As indicated in this passage many of the sacrifices of Seth's sacred animals were by fire.[3] Such sacrifices were outside the official temple ritual as we know it. In fact one Ptolemaic text definitely states that 'the pig shall be slaughtered and laid upon the altar of burnt-sacrifice of the river bank. An altar of earth shall be made for it.'[4] The Ptolemaic texts are of an Osirian complexion, and they look upon that merely as a complete destruction of the enemy. But in reality that was only a transferred explanation given by the new religion. Actually burning was the method proper for the sacrifice *of* the old sky- and fertility-god, though the Osiris-worshippers considered it a sacrifice of the enemy *to* their own fertility-god.

Sesoosis-Sesostris has figured largely in this study, and his son Pherôs does so also. Pherôs' story shows many features of the sky-fertility-religion. He attempted to control the storm and the Nile; he was smitten with blindness, an affliction to which rainmakers are liable (pp. 76, 77); the

---

[1] Grapow, *Religiöse Urkunden*, II, p. 128, Abschnitt 8 of ch. xviii of the Book of the Dead.

[2] Junker in *ZÄS*, XLVIII, p. 75. [3] Id. *op. cit.* pp. 74–6.

[4] Id. *op. cit.* p. 75.

only person able to assist him was a woman, the wife of a gardener (κηπουρός), i.e. a cultivator of the soil. His story ends in a holocaust of adulteresses at the 'city' or 'village' called 'Red Soil' ('Ερυθρὴ βῶλος, Hdt. II, 111) or 'Sacred Soil' (Diod. I, 59). The epithets 'red' and 'sacred' suggest a connexion with Seth; adultery is a too great exuberance in the cause of fertility, and the death was by fire, as so often in these stories.

Heliodorus, the novelist of the third century A.D., supposed that a firewalking ceremony was still held in Ethiopia. The sacred fire had to be brought from the temple by young children, for only they could touch it without harm. That is to say it was liable to be dangerous for those who had reached the age of puberty. In fact it was the virtue of the fire that it burned those who were unchaste, but let the pure pass through in safety.[1] At the Thunderbolt-city of Letopolis there was already by the early Eighteenth Dynasty 'that Night of reckoning the transgressors, that is the Night of Fire for the Adversaries'. The devout Egyptian hoped to be able to say 'I come forth and I go in in the devouring fire on the day of the repelling of rebels in Letopolis',[2] but it is not indicated whether the purity required was sexual or ritual. Of an earlier date still, a late Predynastic trench full of ashes was found at Gerzah.[3] It was 83 inches long, 22 inches wide, and was cut 25 inches

---

[1] Heliodorus, *Aethiopica*, x, §§ 8, 9. Compare the action of the rain-stones among the Madi of the White Nile. Contact with them should be avoided by adults, for apart from being dangerous in a general way (Rogers in *Man*, 1927, p. 83) they are specifically dangerous sexually, *loc. cit.* pp. 82, 86, and cf. p. 84, where one's children would die.

[2] Wainwright in *JEA*, XVIII, pp. 164-7.

[3] Petrie, Wainwright and Mackay, *The Labyrinth, Gerzeh and Mazghuneh*, p. 8, and Pl. xiii, no. 108. Ashes were buried in great quantities with the dead in Predynastic Egypt.

deep into the rock. It contained nothing at all but the ashes and three finger, or possibly toe, bones. Was it for a fire-walking ceremony?

But let us continue the case of the adulteresses. Seeing that the fire was the proper means of sacrificing the spirit of fertility, and that an adulteress is one in whom this spirit is emphatically incarnate, it is natural that death by fire should become the normal punishment for adultery in Egypt.[1] It was a case of making the punishment fit the crime, and of killing two birds with one stone; of securing a suitable victim and of executing a criminal at the same time. The same principle has already been seen at work; in the case of Seth-Typhon's sacred animals who were negligent in their duty (p. 32), and again in the story of Bocchoris, where a rival was disposed of and the demands of religion satisfied (pp. 39–41). Death by fire was meted out to the unfaithful wife of Ubaoner, who was supposed to have lived in the time of Nebka of the Third Dynasty.[2] Further, her ashes were cast into the river. This is a wide-spread method of dealing with the ashes of the fertility

---

[1] Death by fire seems to have been specially connected with the sky-gods, for it is twice demanded for offenders against Amûn. In the reign of Psametik I it was demanded that the priests who had committed murder in the temple of Amûn at el Hibah should be cast into the furnace (Griffith, *Catalogue of the Demotic Papyri in the Rylands Library at Manchester*, III, p. 91, ll. 10–12. For the murder see p. 87, l. 8). In the same century certain priests in the temple of Amûn of Napata (Gebel Barkal) in Ethiopia had planned to kill an innocent man. For this wickedness the god 'slew them and they were made into a burnt-offering' (Schäfer in *Klio*, VI, pp. 291, 292; cf. also pp. 63, 64 *infra*).

[2] Westcar Papyrus, probably written in the Hyksos period, *c.* 1788–1580 B.C., Erman, *The Literature of the Ancient Egyptians* (trans. Blackman), pp. 37, 38. Under the name Nitocris the courtesan, Rhodopis-Nitocris, is similarly said to have burned herself alive, see p. 41.

victim,[1] and on p. 74 it will be seen that the ashes of the Seth-sacrifices were treated as a rain-charm. Ubaoner's wife clearly served as a sacrifice of the Old Religion, just as the adulteresses did in the story of Pherôs. Such victims could have served as substitutes for the king, the proper victim, if so desired, or they might have been merely supernumeraries.

The story has already been told (pp. 47 ff.) of the escape of Sesoosis-Sesostris from the fire in which he ought to have met his end. Herodotus, II, 107, says that two of his sons laid down their lives in the flames in order to secure his escape from them. Diodorus, I, 57, is less explicit, merely implying that with the exception of the king himself the whole family perished. The death of the sons and the escape of the king is entirely comparable to the legend of the king of Sweden, one of whose sons was sacrificed every ninth year to let him escape (p. 50). The Sesostris story looks like a memory of the sacrifice of substitutes for the king, and the manner of their death was that of the Seth victims at Nekheb-Eileithyiapolis. Something of this sort seems to have originated the superficially extraordinary story of the treatment accorded by Cambyses to the mummy of his predecessor Amasis. Herodotus, III, 16, says that he had it ill-treated and finally burned, 'but the Egyptians say, it was not Amasis that was thus treated, but some other

---

[1] In France the ashes of the effigy called Shrove Tuesday were thrown into the sea, and at Saint-Lô the effigy was set on fire and cast into the river, Frazer, *The Dying God*, pp. 229, 230. Joan of Arc was burned at the stake as a 'witch' and her ashes were cast into running water, M. A. Murray, *The Witch-cult in Western Europe*, p. 276. In Germany a condemned 'witch' asked that her ashes should be strewn on water 'lest being scattered in the air they should breed clouds, drought and hail', id. *The God of the Witches*, p. 136; Grimm, *Teutonic Mythology* (trans. Stallybrass), p. 1087, where this is quoted and much more to do with storm-raising.

Egyptian....For they say, that Amasis, having been informed by an oracle of what should happen to him after death, in order to remedy the impending evil, buried the body of this very man, who was scourged, near the door of his own sepulchre....' But Herodotus does not believe it, thinking the Egyptians falsely boasted of these instructions. Here, however, is a definite substitute, and one not only provided as the result of an oracle, but also consumed by fire as were the Seth-sacrifices.

It has already been pointed out that Plutarch and Diodorus tell how the kings of Egypt used to offer up living men as burnt sacrifices, and the Sacaea in Babylon has given details of how a Mock King is set up. Originally this was done in all seriousness, and the Mock King suffered as a vicarious sacrifice, giving his life for his king and country. But as time went on he has been allowed to enact his own death by fire. By modern times this has been progressively degraded, until today the Mock King has in many countries merely become a comic figure, the centre of annual festivities, known in Europe as King Carnival, the Lord of Misrule, or sim. The festival often ends in some such manner as the conducting of the Mock King to the fire, through which he jumps leaving his royalty, i.e. his insignia, to be consumed in the flames.[1] Sometimes he is burned in effigy.[2] Sometimes it even comes down to burning nothing at all,

[1] As at Aachen, Frazer, *Balder the Beautiful*, I, p. 120.

[2] After being stripped of his finery King Carnival is burned in effigy at Frosinone in south Italy (Frazer, *The Dying God*, p. 223), and at Auxerre in France after having been stripped of her finery the Corn Mother is burned to ashes in the form of the last sheaf (id. *Spirits of the Corn and of the Wild*, I, p. 135). In Bohemia the effigy of a witch used to be burned in the bonfire on the eve of May Day, i.e. at the great festival of the Old Religion, Walpurgis Night (id. *Balder the Beautiful*, I, p. 159). Many other burnings of effigies are quoted in *The Dying God*, pp. 224–33.

but merely to a pretence at burning the living victim.[1] The last relic of all is when there is not even a pretence at burning anything of any sort, but the bonfires are lighted with a view to bring blessing on the fields, or merely to burn or drive away whatever witches there may be in the neighbourhood.[2] Thus, the escape of the victim through the fire is a known amelioration of the old sacrifice.

Tradition would show that this easing of conditions was known in ancient Egypt. As has been seen, p. 48, Sesostris escaped through the fire that had been lighted by his would-be successor with a view to consume him. There was also a story that Anysis-Bocchoris did not perish in the flames, but finally came forth from the ashes collected around him, p. 39. As a matter of fact this very piece of play-acting was still being carried out in every little town in Upper Egypt as recently as sixty or seventy years ago. On the Coptic New Year's Day a villager assumed the role of governor taking the title of Abu Nerûz, 'Father of the New Year', and a special costume. The authority of this mock king had become a burlesque; a carnival. It lasted for three days, when 'at length he, that is his dress, is condemned to death by burning, and from the ashes creeps out the slavish Fellah'.[3] That the festival takes place in accordance with the Coptic, not the Muslim, calendar, is enough to make its antiquity probable. But we can go further than that. Plutarch says[4] of the former burning alive of the men

[1] Frazer, *Balder the Beautiful*, I, pp. 148, 152, 155, 159, 186; cf. also p. 160; II, pp. 25 ff.
[2] Id. *op. cit.* I, pp. 157, 159, 160.
[3] Klunzinger, *Upper Egypt*, p. 185; Rifaud, *Voyage en Égypte, en Nubie, etc.* Pl. 46, from which Pl. II is reproduced. Cf. also Murray in *Man*, 1914, No. 12; id. in *Ancient Egypt*, 1921, pp. 79 ff.; Petrie in *Ancient Egypt*, 1924, p. 97, and a portion of Rifaud's plate.
[4] *De Iside et Osiride*, § 73.

representing Seth-Typhon at Eileithyiapolis-Nekheb-el-Kab that 'this used to be carried out publicly and at one proper time in the Dog-days'. The Dog-days are those round about the Rising of Sirius, and that marked the New Year in the ancient Egyptian calendar. Hence, the ancient Seth sacrifices were burned at the New Year, just as in the nineteenth century Abu Nerûz' insignia of office was still burned at the New Year. Both took place in Upper Egypt, so that the Abu Nerûz carnival ending in the flames was the last remnant of the ancient sacrifice by fire of men representing Seth-Typhon. The history of the ceremony has thus been one of continuous degradation; first the king himself was burned alive as the earthly incarnation of Seth, next a human substitute for the king, then merely the insignia of office in a burlesque carnival, and now at last even that has perhaps ceased within the last two generations. It was a fertility-festival, agricultural produce in the form of bunches of dates being carried in Abu Nerûz' procession.

It has already been shown (pp. 20, 21) that the *sed*-festival was a fertility-rite, hence it would be the sort of occasion when sacrifice might be expected. Foreigners, and especially prisoners of war, all the world over have provided an obvious supply of substitutes, and in Egypt the Busiris story concerns the sacrifices of foreigners to the sky-god. Hence, it may be pointed out that from our earliest example the *sed*-festival was at times connected with a victorious campaign. At Narmer's *sed* 120,000 captives were represented.[1] The statues of Khasekhem show the king robed for the *sed*-festival, and large numbers of overthrown enemies at his feet.[2] Pepi I's tablet commemorates both his *sed*-

[1] Quibell and Petrie, *Hierakonpolis*, I, Pl. xxvi, B.
[2] Id. *op. cit.* Pls. xxxix, xl, xli.

Plate II

ABU NERÛZ CARNIVAL

festival and his conquest of Sinai.[1] Mentuhotep I smites a 'chieftain of Libya' and is accompanied by two men bearing the door-pivots.[2] He, therefore, does this at a *sed*-festival. Hatshepsut as a sphinx tramples enemies in the presence of the usual group of *sed*-festival symbols,[3] while Merenptah,[4] Neos Dionysos,[5] and Tiberius[6] are also accompanied by this group of symbols when they slaughter their enemies.[7] Remains of prisoners with their arms tied behind them are to be seen in the bottom row of what is evidently part of a *sed*-festival scene of Amenhotep III's.[8] But whether these captives were sacrifices, and whether they were in any way substitutes for the king himself, must remain a subject for future investigation. In any case there is no sign of their being put to death by fire.

There is of course yet another way of avoiding the extreme penalty of kingship. This is by magic. The purpose of the sacrifice being magical, it came to be appreciated that magic would serve to renew the failing powers of the reigning king. In this connexion Moret has pointed out that one of the purposes of the *sed*-festival was for the renewal of life in the Pharaoh.[9] Seligman emphasizes this by pointing to the frequency with which the festival was

---

[1] Gardiner and Peet, *The Inscriptions of Sinai*, Pl. viii, 16.
[2] Bissing-Bruckmann, *Denkmäler*, Pl. 33, A, b (Lieferung 6).
[3] Naville, *Deir el Bahari*, Pl. clx.
[4] Petrie, *The Palace of Apries*, Pl. xxi.
[5] *L. D.* IV, Pls. 51, b, 52, a.   [6] *L. D.* IV, Pl. 74, c.
[7] Sahurê's sculptures include among other things the remains of a *sed*-festival and of a victorious campaign. This may be only chance, for there is nothing to connect them together.
[8] *L. D.* III, Pl. 85, c.
[9] *Du caractère religieux de la royauté pharaonique*, pp. 255, 258; *Mystères égyptiens*, p. 86 (published in *Anns. du musée Guimet, Bibliothèque de Vulgarisation*, tome XXXVII (1912), *Conférences faites au musée Guimet*); *From Tribe to Empire*, p. 152; *The Nile and Egyptian Civilization*, pp. 128, 129.

celebrated as old age came on, especially in the cases of Amenhotep III and Ramesses II. He also shows that such rejuvenation ceremonies are common in Africa today.[1]

Events concerned with the kingship in Ethiopia have been mentioned a number of times. There was the subservience of the Libyo-Ethiopian kings to Amûn. There were also the facts that Ergamenes rebelled against his fate in the third century B.C., and that this resulted in his slaughtering the priests. Yet again there was the piety of another king of Ethiopia, Sabacon, nearly five hundred years earlier, and an interesting milestone in religious progress lies in the story which Herodotus and Diodorus tell of him. Diodorus, I, 65, says that 'the god in Thebes', i.e. the sky-god Amûn, appeared to him. He told him that 'he would not be able to rule over Egypt prosperously or for a long time, unless he should pass through with his retinue cutting the priests in halves', and this advice was often repeated. But Sabacon dared not do so. Herodotus, II, 139, tells the same story but in less detail, though he gives the important information that Sabacon had been assigned a definite length of reign by the Ethiopian oracle. This clearly means that in due time the priesthood of the sky-religion would demand his life in sacrifice, as we know they did of Ergamenes. The thought occurred to Sabacon of saving himself by destroying them. But the time was not yet ripe for such a proceeding. It took another five hundred years before public opinion in Ethiopia would be sufficiently advanced to enable the king, in the person of Ergamenes, to carry out such a *coup d'état*.[2]

[1] *Egypt and Negro Africa*, pp. 52, 53–6.

[2] There is no question of the historical action of Ergamenes having given rise to an apocryphal story about the earlier Sabacon. Herodotus' account of Sabacon's temptation was already in writing some one hundred and fifty years before Ergamenes' reign.

In the next century after Sabacon a curious thing took place at Napata (Gebel Barkal), the capital of Ethiopia. It can, however, probably be explained by what we now know of divine fertility-kings. Certain men in the temple of Amûn there 'had planned in their hearts to kill a man in whom there was no fault, and the god had not commanded it to be done'. The god was so offended that he 'slew them, and they were made into a burnt-offering, in order to instil fear into all prophets and priests, who carry the splendid god, before the greatness of his might and the extent of his power'. His majesty then addressed 'all prophets and all priests who do evil in the temples'.[1]

Murder must have been common enough in Ethiopia to call for no special comment except from the bereaved relatives. Yet here no murder had been committed, but the mere intention to do so was severely punished, and the occasion was sufficiently important for it to be commemorated on a large stela. It could, therefore, have been no ordinary murder that was contemplated. Amûn resented the intention because he had not commanded the death, as he evidently sometimes did. He avenged the insult to himself by having the priests put to death as sacrifices in the fire—that is to say in the manner of fertility victims.

Who was the unnamed man whom the priests designed to do to death without cause? Could it have been the king? Could it be that Ergamenes was not the first in Ethiopia to take action against the priests of Amûn, and that this seventh century king did what in the eighth century Sabacon had been tempted to, but dared not, do? It was done as a lesson to the priests. The king had incurred

[1] Schäfer, *Die sogenannte 'Stèle de l'excommunication' aus Napata* in *Klio*, VI, p. 291.

the hatred of some powerful party in the land, for his face and names have been obliterated from the sculpture.

However, if it were indeed the king who was aimed at, it may not have been that he was revolting from his lawful fate, for it was early in his reign that he struck—in his second year. It, therefore, might have been that the priests had quarrelled with him, and had made accusations against him which, if true, would have merited his death. In fact he speaks of the intended victim as being blameless of an unnamed fault. What could such a fault have been? If it were the king who was in question, it would surely have been a failure to produce rain, good harvests, and victory in war. This indeed entails the direst punishment, as has already been seen (pp. 1, 32, 33). To take the life of a fertility-king at the appointed time and in the appointed manner is to offer the highest sacrifice; to take it before the time and in any other manner, unless as a punishment for failure, is to commit the foulest possible murder, indeed to strike at the prosperity of the whole country.

Having seen the sort of thing that had at one time gone on in Egypt and its effect on two Ethiopian kings, we may well ask whether something similar did not underlie the religious history of the Old Kingdom. Archaeologically we know it was a time of change. At Abydos Petrie found a layer of ashes containing burnt offerings, which consisted of hundreds of little twists of clay.[1] It dates to the Old

---

[1] *Abydos*, II, pp. 9, 10, 30, 48, and Pl. xiv, 285–7. Cf. the great pyre of Hercules on Mount Oeta in Thessaly, consisting of a thick bed of ashes including a variety of offerings, Pappadakis in *Bull. de Corr. hell.* 1920, p. 392; 1921, p. 523. It has already been mentioned on pp. 55, 56 that a hitherto unexplained fire ceremony had been carried out in Late Predynastic days in the cemetery at Gerzah, Petrie, Wainwright and Mackay, *The Labyrinth, Gerzeh and Mazghuneh*, p. 8, and Pl. xiii, 108.

Kingdom. As it is also unique in Egyptian archaeology, it indicates some sort of change in the methods of sacrifice. Also the Old Kingdom saw the establishment of sun-worship as the religion of the kings, and this is a religion which does not require the sacrifice demanded by the old one. The change was slow and halting. For instance, all through the Fifth and Sixth Dynasties it was only very occasionally that the kings called themselves 'Son of the Sun', and it was not until the Eleventh Dynasty that the use of this title became regular. Much has been seen of Seth, an important god of the Old Religion. At the end of the Second Dynasty there had been a great resurgence of his worship under the Seth-king Persabsen. This was suppressed by the Horus-king Khasekhem, who took the dual titles and form of his name 'The Horus and Seth king, Khasekhemui'.[1] This unsuccessful effort on the part of the Seth-kings took place at the time that Rê-worship first begins to appear. It was succeeded in the Third Dynasty by that advance of Rê-worship,[2] which in the Fourth Dynasty culminated under Cheops and Chephren, when the Old Religion received its first definite setback. These two kings built their vast pyramids, changed the style of sacrifice, and went down in story as being irreligious. But at the end of the dynasty it was the Old Religion's turn once more, and it gained a complete victory over Mycerinus and Shepseskaf. In fact the movement seems to have been the same as Akhenaton's,[3] away from the Old Religion towards Rê-worship. But while the early movement was long drawn out and gradual Akhenaton's failed after the one lifetime. Mycerinus and Shepseskaf had

[1] Newberry in *Ancient Egypt*, 1922, pp. 40–6. Whereas Khasekhem means 'The Power is Manifest', Khasekhemui means 'The Two Powers are Manifest'.

[2] For the rise of Rê-worship see pp. 95–98.

[3] See p. 66 note 1 and pp. 82, 83.

to go back to the Old Religion just as Tutankhaton had to later on.

It has already been seen, and will be seen again (pp. 46, 67), that, though very unwilling, Mycerinus had to submit to his fate in his seventh year, and that this was announced to him by the oracle of Wazet-Buto. His successor Shepseskaf would have nothing to do with Rê; neither mentioning this god in his name; nor building a sun-temple; nor even a pyramid which was a sun-symbol. On the contrary he returned to the old pre-Pyramid form of a mastabah for his tomb,[1] and according to tradition seems to have died in his seventh year (p. 70) like many a king of the Old Religion, or his substitute, all the world over. In the middle of the next dynasty Neuserrê compounded with the rival systems. He did everything possible to magnify Rê; including his name in his own; building him a splendid temple; and being perhaps the first to call himself 'Son of the Sun'.[2] Yet he

---

[1] Now known as Mastabet Fara'un, Jéquier, *Le mastabat Faraoun*, pp. 21, 32, 36. On pp. 36, 37 Jéquier compares the reaction of Shepseskaf to that of Akhenaton. This is of course natural and just. But it should be emphasized that the two were not analogous, being in fact the opposite of each other. While Akhenaton revolted from Amûn, representing the Old Religion, and sought refuge in Rê, Shepseskaf had turned his back on Rê and submitted to the Old Religion. Moreover, the present argument suggests that Shepseskaf's movement was not the flight that Jéquier suggests from an overweening Heliopolitan clergy, whose power threatened to subordinate that of the king. On the contrary, the suggestion is that it was a failure, or possibly an unwillingness, of the king to avail himself of the personal benefits to be gained by adherence to them. Shepseskaf's movement would thus be more like Tutankhaton's (see p. 83) than Akhenaton's. Moreover, while in Akhenaton's case the clergy of the Old Religion were undoubtedly overbearing, it is here suggested that in the Old Kingdom the clergy of Rê had been advancing in power through the patronage of the king.

[2] Gauthier, *Le livre des rois*, I, p. 127. The possible exceptions are Khafrê and Sahurê, id. *op. cit.* pp. 89, 90, 112.

had to accept his seven lives from the death-god, Anubis, under the supervision of Wazet-Buto, whose oracle had allotted the same span of life to Mycerinus. The struggle, which we know archaeologically was going on in the Old Kingdom, finds utterance in Spells 570 and 571 of the Pyramid Texts. Here, in §§ 1453 and 1467, it is said that 'Pepi escapeth the day of death even as Seth escaped his day of death'. Hence it is clear that by the Sixth Dynasty there had been some Pharaohs who had succeeded in escaping the death of Seth, and Pepi intended to be one of them, if it were possible. More than two thousand years later the memory of the struggle reached Herodotus, though in legendary, scarcely historical, form. His stories of the Fourth Dynasty kings show Khufu and Khafrê, like Ergamenes and recent Negro kings, as having had some success in a struggle with the old system. Menkaurê, on the contrary, seems to have had to submit like Sabacon in the story, who was tempted to, but dared not, resist.

Herodotus' remarks may be epitomized thus. Among much else he says that Cheops and Chephren shut up the temples and 'forbade the Egyptians to offer sacrifice' (II, 124, 127). This resulted in all sorts of calamities (128), and the wearing of the people down to the last extremity (129). But the kings lived long (128, 133). Mycerinus, on the other hand, 'made the most righteous judgments', was beneficent, 'opened the temples' and 'permitted the people to return to sacrifices' (129). Yet a message from Buto informed this religious king that he should die in the seventh year, and to this he had to submit, though very unwillingly according to Herodotus (133). His successor was the above-mentioned Shepseskaf, who is known to have been entirely under the influence of the Old Religion. Mycerinus' objection definitely stated that his predecessors 'who had paid no regard to the gods...had lived long; whereas he who was religious must die so soon' (133). Thus, the struggle revolved around sacrifices and ended in the death of a king at a stated time on instructions from the priests, and the time itself is significant. The absence of the sacrifices entailed calamities. The king, who allowed the sacrifices once more, gained a reputation as the most just of kings and he had to die in his seventh year.[1] The parallel with Bocchoris is obvious, as it is, though in less detail, with Nitocris, Sesostris, Busiris, and Sabacon. Yet again, the parallel is also obvious with the well-known doom of royalty under the old sky- and fertility-religion. As with the fertility-king Pherôs (p. 55) the subject of fertility is not absent from these stories of the Fourth Dynasty Pharaohs. Herodotus, II, 126, says that Cheops prostituted his own daughter in a brothel, and that according to one view Mycerinus' pyramid was built by a courtesan (134), who may really have represented a Typhonian queen (pp. 42, 45). Herodotus, not understanding the theory of all this, tells the story of Mycerinus' fate in the form of a complaint by him. He may indeed have made one, seeing that the breakaway had already begun, but if so it failed, and he had to submit in the end. The gods in question were clearly those of the Old Religion. Cheops and Chephren were wicked, paid no regard to them, and lived long; Mycerinus, on the other hand, was obedient to them and died early—in his seventh year, as has many another victim in many a land.

[1] There is thus a deeper reason for the stories than Spiegelberg's supposition (*The Credibility of Herodotus' Account of Egypt*, p. 22) that the legendary wickedness of the Fourth Dynasty kings was due, and in exact proportion, to the size of their pyramids. The size of these buildings may, however, have come to represent an ocular proof of the correctness of the legends.

Though much less definite, similarly queer possibilities may perhaps be collected about another legendary king of this age. This is Sasychis, who like Bocchoris came down in story as one of the six lawgivers of Egypt (Diod. i, 94). Bocchoris 'was a wise sort of man and conspicuous for his craftiness. He drew up all the regulations concerning the kings', while Sasychis was 'a man of unusual understanding' and 'in particular laid down with the greatest precision the rites to be used in honouring the gods'. While Bocchoris undertook the burden of kingship under the ancient sky-fertility-religion and was sacrificed by fire in his seventh year, we find that Sasychis was also concerned with the sky. Diodorus, *loc. cit.*, goes on to tell us that besides being meticulous about religious rites, he also 'taught his countrymen both to speculate about the stars and to observe them'. The care for religion is conspicuous in the legends of two other of our kings. Thus, Mycerinus 'made the most righteous judgments', and was religious, and had to die in his seventh year. Sabacon 'much excelled his predecessors in piety and uprightness' and 'he would not be able to rule over Egypt prosperously or for a long time, unless he should pass through with his retinue cutting the priests in halves'. It has often been suggested that the Sasychis of Diodorus is the Asychis of Herodotus (II, 136), in which case he would probably belong to the Old Kingdom, for Herodotus puts him next after Mycerinus. If so, Sasychis may be a version of the historical Shepseskaf, who was Menkaurê's successor.[1] This successor of Menkaurê is called Sebercheres in

---

[1] Suggested by Lauth, Lieblein and Wiedemann. For references to their identifications and the various others see Gauthier, *Le livre des rois*, I, p. 101, note 1. Hall, *The Ancient History of the Near East* (7th ed.), p. 127, also accepts this view. For Shepseskaf as immediate successor to Menkaurê, see Gauthier in *Anns. Serv.* xxv, pp. 179, 180.

Africanus' copy of Manetho, and is said to have reigned seven years.[1] We have already seen (p. 66) that under Shepseskaf the Old Religion was completely in the ascendant. But, no doubt as a result of the royal impulse towards Rê, this king's funerary cult was dropped almost at once, and officially he was forgotten for nearly a thousand years. Then, in the Middle Kingdom a colony of lower-class people began to have themselves buried under the shadow of his tomb, and his worship was suddenly revived by a mere butcher called Ptahhotep.[2] Here we have evidence that for some reason the king was remembered by the populace in the Middle Kingdom long after his death, and yet again some two thousand years after that, when Herodotus and Diodorus reported the tales they heard told of long ago. It thus seems possible that at the appointed time Shepseskaf took upon himself the supreme sacrifice of the Old Religion like Mycerinus, Bocchoris, and Nitocris, and like them was honoured for it for all time in the memory of the populace, if

[1] The baneful number seven occurs as the length of two reigns on the fragments of the Turin Papyrus which belong to the late Fourth and early Fifth Dynasties. The name of one of the kings is lost, but the *ka* of the other remains. One of the seven-year reigns, therefore, belongs either to Shepseskaf or to Userkaf, both of whom were subject to the Old Religion. During the Third Dynasty the Turin fragments also show two kings between Zoser and Sneferu as reigning six years each. They also show the predecessor of Khafrê as reigning eight years, as they do Neuserrê's successor, Menkauhor (E. Meyer, *Aegyptische Chronologie*, Table facing p. 145, published in *Abhandl. der K. Preuss. Ak. der Wiss.*, 1904, *Phil. hist. Klasse*). Nitocris, whose story has been discussed, is given six years by Eratosthenes, though Manetho, according to Africanus, gave her twelve (Meyer, *op. cit.*, Table facing p. 166, or Dindorf, pp. 195, 108). The story of Mycerinus shows that six years may represent a reign of six years with death in the seventh. Hence, eight years may represent a reign of the full seven years with death in the eighth.

[2] Jéquier in *Comptes rendus de l'acad. des inscr. et belles lettres* (Paris), 1925, pp. 257, 258.

not by the kings who wished to avoid the Old Religion or by the priests of the New.

As a result of all this there can be no doubt that at some early date the kings had had to make the ancient sacrifice and to lay down their lives for the good of their people. The reason was to ensure that their rainmaking powers should pass in their full potency to a virile successor. In Libya the chiefs evidently still had to do so at least as late as the eighth century B.C., and in Ethiopia as late as the third century B.C. In Egypt itself a recrudescence of the old custom was possible under Libyan influences even as late as the eighth century B.C. At one time the method of sacrifice had clearly been by fire, as so often elsewhere. But the existence of royal mummies shows that in historic times the Pharaohs did not ordinarily perish by fire. Equally the lengths of their reigns show that they did not ordinarily lay down their lives at stated intervals. No doubt one or other of the various methods of substitution had early been adopted. There is evidence to suggest that the Fourth Dynasty was a period of struggle for a change of procedure.

All of this has its roots in the remotest past before the people had drifted into the Nile Valley; when they were still living in Libya, and were dependent for their water upon the rain, not upon the Nile. But from this period we have no direct evidence; our material is not from Libya, but from the Nile Valley. It is thus vestigial. Not only had theological thought developed along more cultured lines, but even the physical conditions of life had changed. The result was that not only did the old barbarous customs tend to become softened, but the old forms had to be adapted to the new conditions of dependence upon the Nile, not upon the rain. Signs of this adaptation are not lacking. In the First Dynasty Den-Udymu performs the ancient running

ceremony, and seems at the same time to record the opening
of the dykes for the inundation, cf. p. 25. It is said of Tethmosy III 'Menkheperrê is in the sky like the Moon; the Nile
is at his service; he openeth its cavern to give life to Egypt'.[1]
Though the king appears to be dead, as Drioton supposes,
it is evidently thought that he would continue his beneficent
work for Egypt. We already know that Ramesses II was
credited with power over the elements (pp. 14, 15), and as

Tablet of Den-Udymu.

will now be seen over the subterranean waters of the Nile
also. When he decided to dig a well in the desert it is said of
him on the Kubban stele: 'If thou sayest to the water:
"Come upon the mountain", the flood comes forth quickly
after thy word...'; 'But if thou thyself say to thy father
Hapi, the father of the gods: "Let water be brought upon
the mountain", he will do according to all that thou hast
said,...'; 'The water which is in the nether world hearkens

[1] Drioton in *Egyptian Religion*, 1933, p. 40.

to him (Ramesses II), when he digs water upon the mountain...'.[1] In performing the harvest festival upon earth, Ramesses III cut a sheaf of the primitive emmer-wheat, *bd·t*, before Min, the ancient sky- and fertility-god,[2] but in the next world he expected to reap his own corn before Hapi, the deified inundation of the Nile.[3] A mythical king, called Pherôs (Hdt. II, 111) or a second Sesoosis (Diod. I, 59), is said to have attempted to control both the inundation of the Nile, and the storm of wind which arose at that time. He did it by casting his javelin into the river. This was clearly a magical act, for before crossing a ford a Galla strikes the ground with the handle of his lance; to exorcise the genius of the river as the recorder of the custom supposes.[4] Besides this, sacred spears are prominent in the rain ceremonies of the tribes of the Upper Nile.[5] In fact one Bari rainmaker had 'a two-headed spear used in attacking hostile rain-clouds',[6] and thus treated them just as Pherôs treated the hostile river. Elsewhere we hear of a double

---

[1] B. *A.R.* III, §§ 288, l. 17; 289, ll. 21, 22; 292, l. 35. Seti's inscription recording the digging of a similar well only includes the quite colourless remarks that 'the god led him' and 'the god has performed my petition', id. *op. cit.* III, §§ 170–2. There is perhaps a memory of some such doctrine about the fertility-ruler, Nitocris (p. 41), for she opened the underground waters, Hdt. II, 100. Similarly the underground waters figure in the tale of Cheops (Hdt. II, 127), though he struggled against the fate of this type of king.

[2] Wilkinson, *M and C*, Pl. lx, facing p. 354; Rosellini, *Monumenti del Culto (I Monumenti dell' Egitto e della Nubia*, III), Pl. lxxxvi.

[3] Capart and Werbrouck, *Thebes*, p. 314, fig. 233. Unfortunately the corn is not named either *sw·t* or *bd·t*.

[4] Cerulli in *Harvard African Studies*, 1922, p. 199.

[5] Hastings, *Encyclopaedia of Religion and Ethics*, s.v. Bantu, p. 359; Seligman, *Pagan Tribes*, pp. 403, Nuba; 80, Shilluk; 181, Dinka; 476, Beli; 281, 285, 287, Bari; 330, 331, 341, Lotuko; 129, Acholi. One of the Dinka sacred spears fell from heaven like a falling star, Johnston in *Sudan Notes and Records*, 1934, p. 127.

[6] Seligman in *JRAI*, 1928, p. 469.

sacrifice to stop a famine and to restore fertility to the land. In the first place an oracle instructed the Pharaoh Aegyptus that he should sacrifice his daughter, which he did. This sounds like a memory of a sacrifice of a substitute in the manner of the ancient sky- and fertility-religion. But later the king laid down his own life, and this definitely to the newer giver of plenty, for he cast himself into the Nile.[1] Plutarch says (§ 73, and cf. pp. 33, 53, 60 *supra*) that the Egyptians used to sacrifice by fire men representing Seth-Typhon, the old storm-god, and that 'they used to scatter and dispose of their ashes by winnowing'. To winnow is to toss in the air, hence the ashes of the Seth-sacrifices were scattered in the air. It has already been seen (p. 34 and note 1) that this is a common form of magic for producing rain and promoting the fertility of the fields. However, the ancient rainmaking ceremony had clearly been adapted to the newer conditions demanding a good inundation of the Nile. For Plutarch goes on to say that the sacrifice 'used to be carried out publicly and at one proper time in the Dog-days', that is to say at the rising of Sirius. Now Sirius has nothing to do with rain in Egypt, but does herald the inundation of the Nile.

Both Aegyptus and Pherôs are interesting in another way. Aegyptus, we are told, was another name for the 'Sethos, who is also Ramesses' of the Pelusium story.[2] Therefore, the story just quoted of Aegyptus is yet another one of Ramesses II who, as we know, actually claimed power in the air and over the Nile waters as well. Pherôs was the son

[1] Pseudo-Plutarch, *De Fluviis: Nilus*, published in Teubner's Plutarch, *Moralia*, VII, p. 308. The oracle is said to be the Pythian, and the daughter's name Aganippe!

[2] Josephus, *Contra Apionem*, I, § 102. Eusebius also gives 'Ramesses who is also Aegyptus' at the end of his Eighteenth Dynasty, Aucher, II, p. 25.

and successor of the hero of Pelusium whom Herodotus calls Sesostris. As so many of the others, the stories of Aegyptus and Pherôs refer to the Nineteenth Dynasty. It is, therefore, probably no chance that the inscriptions at Silsilah recording the increase of the offerings 'on that day of casting in the Book of the Inundation' all belong to that period. Actually they are dated in the reigns of Ramesses II, Merenptah his son, and Ramesses III.[1] The fact that the ceremony was carried out at Silsilah, not at Aswan, should be noted. Aswan seems to us the frontier where the Nile enters Egypt, and therefore the natural place for the performance of such a ceremony. However, further to the north the cliffs at Silsilah form another frontier to Egypt, for south of this the cultivable strips become so narrow as almost to cease to exist. Newberry has long ago seen reason to suggest[2] that the Scorpion King's realm reached no further south than that. Does the fact that in the New Kingdom the ceremony was performed there imply that it originated in that archaic period? Ancient though it would then be, it would still be far less ancient than the rainmaking ceremony of Libyan times. Thus, there is sufficient to show that the fertility duties of the Pharaohs were double ones, originally concerning the rain but later the Nile. This was the result of the

---

[1] L. D. III, Pls. 175, a, l. 10; 200, d, l. 10; 218, d, last line though much destroyed. The texts have been published and studied by Stern in ZÄS, 1873, pp. 129 ff.; Palanque in Le Nil, pp. 71 ff.; Moret, La mise à mort du dieu en Égypte, pp. 10 ff. In the seventh century A.D. Amru cast in a command to the Nile to rise in the name of Allah, Maqrizi, Description topographique et historique de l'Égypte (translated by U. Bouriant in Méms. Miss. arch. fr. du Caire, XVII), p. 164. The New Kingdom 'Book of the Inundation' would more probably have been a statement of the offerings made, or perhaps a collection of spells.

[2] Newberry and Garstang, A Short History of Ancient Egypt (1904), p. 16.

change which had come over Egyptian farming, since the theory of the ruler's powers had taken form.

There is a curious detail which recurs several times in these stories. It is said that so many of the kings were blind. Anysis-Bocchoris, who either perished in, or escaped from, the flames was blind (Hdt. II, 137), Sesoosis, who escaped the fire, finally became blind (Diod. I, 58), as did Pherôs who tried to control the Nile and the storm (Hdt. II, 111; Diod. I, 59; Pliny, *N.H.* xxxvi, 11 (15)). It will be remembered that blindness was much in evidence at Letopolis, the Thunderbolt-city. The shrewmouse was sacred there because it was thought to be blind, and the name of the god who preceded Horus there was *Mḫnty-n-irty*, 'He who is without eyes'.[1] The commonly accepted story tells how Horus himself was partially blinded by Seth, the storm-god, and the Chester Beatty Papyrus says that the blinding was complete.[2] It can hardly be by chance that this alleged blindness has been inserted in the classical tales of the Egyptian kings. As a matter of fact blindness, such as that attributed to some of the fertility-Pharaohs and to the god of the Thunderbolt-city, and was inflicted by the storm-god, is not peculiar to Egypt, but is found again in modern Africa. There it is a regular part of the sky-religions. Thus, among the Bari of the White Nile the rain-stones are considered bad for the eyes, and one of the rainmakers' eyes were actually bleared.[3] Another Bari rainmaker had to make medicine 'for my (the enquirer's) eyes after witnessing such a wonderful sight' as the rain-stones.[4] On being shown some rain-stones certain old men of the Bari rainmaking

---

[1] Sethe in *Untersuchungen*, x, 164.
[2] For all this see *JEA*, xviii, p. 170.
[3] Seligman in *JRAI*, 1928, p. 468.
[4] Id. in *op. cit.* p. 470.

clan passed them over their eyes.[1] Among the Beli of the Bahr el Ghazal a newly initiated rainmaker is careful to shield his eyes from the rain-stones.[2] This belief probably originates in the blinding nature of the lightning, for among the Madi of the Upper Nile some rain-stones are susceptible to lightning, and have been seen to jump about during a thunderstorm.[3] Among the Zulus an incompetent 'sky-herder', instead of quelling the lightning, finds that the lightning quells him by dazzling his eyes, he becomes afraid, and wishes to go indoors.[4] In fact blindness is the punishment for incompetence in dealing with the storm, and had Horus been more efficient in contending with Seth, he would not have lost his sight or part of it. Hence, the legendary blindness of Anysis-Bocchoris, Sesoosis, and Pherôs provides valuable evidence of the essential correctness of these tales, and is a further scrap of evidence that they refer to sky- and fertility-rites. Yet another point shows the intrinsic worth of the stories. It is that, like the kings of the Old Kingdom and Akhenaton in the New Kingdom, Pherôs turned to the sun-god in his affliction (Diod. I, 59), and this he did by command of Wazet-Buto (Hdt. II, 111).

Another guarantee of their general credibility is that Buto and Nekheb (Eileithyiapolis) figure so largely in them. These were the prehistoric cities of the two patron goddesses

[1] Id. in *op. cit.* p. 464.
[2] Id. *Pagan Tribes*, p. 478. Among the Madi of the White Nile contact with the rain-stones is liable to result in illness and even death, Rogers in *Man*, 1927, pp. 82, 83, 84, 86.
[3] Rogers in *op. cit.* pp. 82, 86. Thunderstones are also susceptible to lightning round the Baltic. Thus, on the approach of thunder they move in Westphalia, C. Blinkenberg, *The Thunderweapon in Religion and Folklore*, p. 96, no. 94 h; they sweat in Westphalia and Schleswig, id. *op. cit.* p. 82, no. 69; p. 96, no. 94 h; they turn red in Esthonia, id. *op. cit.* p. 90, no. 82 m.
[4] Callaway, *The Religious System of the Amazulu*, p. 377.

of the kingship, and their presence once more indicates the extreme antiquity of the customs discussed in this article. The Seth-sacrifice took place at Nekheb, and most of the other incidents took place under directions from Buto. Neuserrê received his seven lives in this way, Mycerinus was granted his lease of life from this city, and it was from here that Pherôs received instructions as to curing his blindness.

Yet another guarantee of their essential reliability is that in the Nineteenth Dynasty it is known that there was a revival of Seth-worship.[1] Hence, it is natural that power over the elements and the subterranean waters should have been ascribed to Ramesses II, and that he should have been considered as the giver of plenty. This also is apparent in the classical stories, so many of which cluster about him as the most famous king of that dynasty, whether under the names of Aegyptus, Sesostris, Sesoosis, or Sethos who is also Ramesses.

Another point which emerges is the continual recurrence of the numbers nine and seven. Both of these are well known in the primitive sky-fertility-religions of the world. Thus, we have already met the Mock King 'Lord of the Heavenly Hosts' in Siam who ploughs the nine ritual furrows, and the mythical king of Sweden who sacrificed nine of his sons at intervals of nine years. To these may be added Minos in Crete who went to Zeus, the sky-god, every ninth year.[2] Besides this, every ninth year he sacrificed strangers in the form of seven youths and seven maidens from Athens, and

---

[1] E.g., Roeder in Roscher's *Lexikon*, s.v. *Set*, cols. 750, 751. At his first *sed*-festival, Ramesses II receives life from Nubti, Wilkinson, *M and C*, Pl. lxiii, facing p. 366. In the Twelfth Dynasty Senusret III had received years from Seth at his *sed*-festival, see Schott's description of the scene in Schäfer's article in Griffith, *Studies*, p. 428.

[2] Roscher, *Lexikon*, s.v. *Minos*, cols. 2995 ff.

this he did to the Minotaur who was also called 'Asterios "The Starry One"'.[1] The great sacrifice still took place in mediaeval France every ninth year, but in England apparently only during Danish times.[2] In mediaeval England the cycle was one of seven years,[3] and nearer to Egypt both in time and place was the well-known seven-year cycle of Israelite agriculture: 'And six years thou shalt sow thy land, and shalt gather in the fruits thereof: But the seventh year thou shalt let it rest and lie still' (Exod. xxiii, 10, 11; Lev. xxv, 3, 4). In Lev. xxv, 8, 10, 11 the system is elaborated into the great cycle of seven times seven years. Similarly the Fourth Commandment applies it to the days: 'Six days shalt thou labour, and do all that thou hast to do; but the seventh day is the Sabbath of the Lord thy God.' David stopped a famine by selecting seven of Saul's sons, who were 'hanged in the hill before the Lord' 'in the days of harvest, in the first days, in the beginning of barley harvest' 'and after that God was intreated for the land' (II Sam. xxi, 1, 6, 9, 14). Both seven and nine appear in the fertility ceremonies of the ancient Persians. At their New Year festivities of Nauruz a dish was brought to the king containing seven ears and nine grains each of wheat, barley, pease, vetches, sesame, and rice. A loaf was made of these grains and eaten by the assembled company.[4]

The cycle of nine is not so common in Egypt as that of seven. Perhaps it may not be native, for apart from the nine kings at Min's harvest festival it has only occurred in an

---

[1] Roscher, *Lexikon*, s.v. *Minotauros*, cols. 3004, 3005. Apparently the period varied in different traditions, some making it a yearly, others a three-yearly, sacrifice.

[2] M. A. Murray, *The God of the Witches*, p. 159.

[3] Id. *op. cit.* pp. 134–5, 159.

[4] J. Richardson, *A Dictionary, Persian, Arabic, and English* (Johnson's ed., 1829), p. 1293, s.v. *māh*.

Asiatic or northern connexion.[1] Sesostris' escape from the flames at Pelusium was made after a period of nine years spent in Asia and even in Europe. It may be noted that both Josephus[2] and Eusebius[3] specify Cyprus as one of the lands visited, for it was a stranger from Cyprus who taught Busiris to sacrifice to Zeus-Amûn after a nine years' drought. A legend tells how 'Shu (the air-god) had departed to heaven: there was no exit from the palace by the space of nine days. Now these [nine] days were in violence and tempest: none whether god or man could see the face of his fellow'.[4] Here again northern influence is apparent, for 'certain Asiatics' are concerned with the story, and certain evil-doers came from the eastern hills invading the eastern part of the Delta. That is the part of the country in which Pelusium is situated. Moreover, the story as it stands comes from the Greek period, like those of Sesostris and Busiris. Another story from the Greek period is that of the blindness of the fertility-king Pherôs. This blindness lasted for nine years, for it was only cured in the tenth (Diod. I, 59).

The usual Egyptian cycle was clearly the sevenfold one.[5] At the harvest festival ceremonies before Min in the New

---

[1] At the Abu Nerûz festival of the high Nile and the Coptic New Year the villagers drink, or bathe in, the new waters nine times, Murray in *Ancient Egypt*, 1921, p. 80. See further, p. 106 *infra*, for the possible differentiation of an Egyptian seven-area and a northern nine-area in very ancient times.

[2] *Contra Apionem*, § 99.   [3] Aucher, I, p. 232.

[4] Griffith, *The Antiquities of Tell el Yahudiyeh, etc.*, Pl. xxv, ll. 7, 8, and p. 72.

[5] In late times seven comes more and more to replace four as a number for every description of magic, Sethe, *Von Zahlen und Zahlworten bei den alten Ägyptern* (Strassburg, 1916), pp. 33–6. Nine scarcely exists before late times, pp. 38, 39. Most of the evidence quoted here is additional to Sethe's. Seven occurs many times in the magic of the Ramesside papyri, Gardiner, *Hieratic Papyri in the Brit. Mus.* (Third Series), I, pp. 58, 59, 61, 68, 71, 119, 125.

Kingdom the priest repeated the formulae seven times while circumambulating the king.[1] Min is escorted by a number of Pharaohs represented by their statues. At Medinet Habu there are seven of them,[2] and at the Ramesseum there are fourteen, i.e. twice seven.[3] Later in the festival nine Pharaohs attend the ceremonial cutting of the sheaf of *bd·t*, emmer-wheat, and the offering of it to Min's White Bull.[4] The mythical famine ascribed to the reign of Zoser lasted for seven years,[5] and in Gen. xli, 1–7 the prospects for the crops and cattle were revealed to Pharaoh in cycles of seven years each. The ancient sky- and fertility-god, Seth, has figured largely in these pages. It is perhaps not mere chance that in his *De Iside et Osiride*, § 31, Plutarch says that Typhon fled out of the battle for seven days on an ass, and in § 30 that in the Pythagorean system Typhon was produced in the even number fifty-six. Fifty-six happens to be a multiple of seven. Similarly in the Nineteenth Dynasty papyrus giving details of Typhonian men, one of the periods of life allotted to them is eighty-four years.[6] This again happens

---

[1] Gauthier, *Les fêtes du dieu Min*, p. 61, ll. 13, 14; p. 227, l. 2.

[2] Champollion, *Monuments*, Pl. ccxiii. For the whole scene see Wilkinson, *M and C*, Pl. lx, facing p. 355, where the seven kings will be found in the centre. [3] L. D. III, Pl. 163.

[4] MEDINET HABU, L. D. III, Pl. 212, a, b = Rosellini, *Monumenti del Culto*, Pl. lxxxvi. For the whole scene, see Wilkinson, *M and C*, Pl. lx, facing p. 355, where the nine kings will be found in the right-hand bottom corner. RAMESSEUM, L. D. III, Pl. 162 = Rosellini, *op. cit.* Pl. lxxvii, where only the last six of the row of kings are left. There is no need to doubt they were originally nine, for the inscription above them leaves room for them, and is identical with that above the nine at Medinet Habu.

[5] De Morgan, *Catalogue des monuments et inscriptions de l'Égypte antique*, I, p. 80, ll. 1, 2. The part that concerns us here is translated by Ranke in Gressmann, *Altorientalische Texte und Bilder zum Alten Testamente* (1909), I, p. 233.

[6] Gardiner, *Hieratic Papyri in the Brit. Mus.* (Third Series), I, p. 20. There were other spans of life for Typhonians, most of which have

to be a multiple of seven. Seven enters largely into the tale of Ubaoner's wife, the adulteress who was treated as a fertility-sacrifice. Her husband made a magic crocodile of wax. It was seven spans long, but came to life as a crocodile of seven cubits, and it held the adulterer for seven days before it devoured him.[1] In the Fourth Dynasty Mycerinus is said to have been granted a lease of life to his seventh year; in the Fifth Dynasty Neuserrê actually received his seven lives from the death-god, Anubis; in the Twenty-Fourth Dynasty Bocchoris reigned six years and, therefore, no doubt suffered his martyrdom in his seventh. One story gives a six years' reign to Nitocris, who was Typhonian in colouring, and the Turin Papyrus gives six years to two kings at the end of the Third Dynasty. This was when the Pharaohs were beginning the struggle against their fate. The same papyrus gives a seven years' reign to each of two kings of the late Fourth and early Fifth Dynasties, while Manetho gives seven years to his Sebercheres who represents Shepseskaf of the Fourth Dynasty. In the same dynasties this papyrus shows Khafrê's predecessor and Neuserrê's successor as reigning eight years each.[2] There is a statement that Sabacon, who sacrificed Bocchoris, himself only reigned eight years. It may well be that these represent a lease of life of seven years, at the end of which the great offering was made.

In their struggle to escape their fate under the old sky-religion, we know that the Fourth Dynasty Pharaohs sought refuge in sun-worship. Likewise it was to the sun-god that

unfortunately perished. The other that has survived is sixty years, which is meaningless here.

[1] Erman, *The Literature of the Ancient Egyptians* (trans. Blackman), pp. 37, 38. Though the word 'spans' has perished the numeral seven is preserved.

[2] See p. 70 note 1 *supra*.

the fertility-king, Pherôs, turned in his affliction.[1] The Eighteenth Dynasty saw another royal revolt from the Old Religion, at that time represented by Amûn. This was under Akhenaton, who like the others turned to sun-worship in his trouble. As with Cheops' and Chephren's, Akhenaton's revolt was shortlived, and the rebels were soon brought back to a sense of duty. In the Eighteenth Dynasty it was Tutankhaton who had to play the part of Mycerinus and Shepseskaf and take upon him the yoke of the sky-god, in his case Amûn. He had to change his name from Tut-ankh-Aton, 'The Life of the Sun's Disc is Pleasing', to Tut-ankh-Amûn, 'The Life of Amûn is Pleasing'.[2] He also had to return to Thebes, Amûn's city, where at his death he was buried. His was a short reign, the ninth being his highest recorded year,[3] and he did not return to Thebes immediately on his accession to the throne. From a variety of evidence Pendlebury has calculated that his death took place seven years after his change of name, return to Thebes, and to allegiance to Amûn.[4] Seven years; a fateful period! All this is extraordinarily suggestive of his having to accept the age-old doom of the divine kings of the sky-fertility-religions all the world over, and having to render up his life for the good of his people. We know that, however he may have died, it was not in the fire. Hence, if his life was taken in the seventh year, he had obtained at least that relief from the utmost rigour of the law. It has been done often enough

---

[1] Diod. I, 59. After his attempt to control the storm and the Nile he was smitten with blindness: 'But in the tenth year an oracular command was given to him to do honour to the god in Heliopolis, etc.'

[2] For this rendering instead of the usual 'Living Image of the Sun's Disc' and 'Amûn', see Gunn in *JEA*, XII, pp. 252, 253.

[3] Carter, *The Tomb of Tut·Ankh·Amen*, III, pp. 21, 22.

[4] Pendlebury, *Tell el-Amarna*, p. 33; 1367 B.C. change of name, 1360 B.C. death and burial at Thebes.

elsewhere, and in Egypt his predecessors had evidently fought for, and won, it long before.

In the Old Kingdom Cheops' and Chephren's movement towards Rê-worship had been succeeded by Mycerinus' and Shepseskaf's return to the Old Religion. Similarly, Akhenaton's movement away from the sky-gods was succeeded by an intense reaction in their favour. The Nineteenth Dynasty was a period when so great an emphasis was laid on the Pharaoh's powers and duties as rainmaker, that stories about them filtered through to the Graeco-Roman world. This great wave of reaction carried Seth to his last triumph, before he fell never to rise again. During this dynasty two kings called themselves Seti, 'Belonging to Seth', and Ramesses II was devoted to the worship of this god. The founder of the next dynasty was called Setnekht, 'Seth is victorious', and at this time private individuals commonly bore names formed upon that of the god. It was Amûn who, at the end of the Eighteenth Dynasty, had won the victory for the old sky-gods about 1360 B.C. Although Seth's triumph was shortlived, Amûn was able to consolidate his, for he was more fortunately placed. His priests held the feeble kings of the later Twentieth Dynasty completely under their tutelage for some seventy years. Then, his high priest, Herihor, usurped the throne as first king of the Twenty-First Dynasty. Some one hundred and fifty years later again immigrants from Libya, the ancient cradle of Egypt's sky-gods, seized the throne of Egypt as the Twenty-Second Dynasty, and about the same time that of Ethiopia also. In both countries they found the sky-religion firmly entrenched in the person of Amûn. Their crude ideas carried the Old Religion to its culminating horror as known to us in history. That was the sacrifice of Bocchoris by his successor Sabacon about 712 B.C.

CONCLUSIONS

THE rainmaking religion is extremely ancient and widespread throughout the world, and the position under it may be briefly stated thus. The king is the central figure. He it is who ensures the well-being of the crops, of the herds, and hence of his people, for he is the incarnation of the spirit of fertility. This makes him divine. The power within him must never be allowed to grow old with his declining years. This tremendous destiny entails all sorts of responsibilities. He has to carry out the necessary rituals to accomplish the above results, the last of which is to render up the power within him intact. This last duty means that he has to commit suicide, or be put to death, while still in his prime. This is unpleasant, and, though even today it is often undertaken willingly and proudly, history is also full of the various attempts to evade it. This means, either that a substitute of some sort is found to die the death, or that the powers, being magical, are rejuvenated by magic. The sky-fertility-religion itself and many of its characteristics may be found in Egypt, where many of the age-old ceremonies had to be adapted to the special local conditions.

Fertility comes from the sky, which fertilizes the earth by rain. Many of the gods of Egypt prove to be sky-gods, storm-gods, fertility-gods, and they go back to the beginning of time there. In fact some of them, or their prototypes, can be traced back to Libyan days before the 'Egyptians' had descended into the Nile Valley. Many were so ancient as to be already dying out in the Old Kingdom. Such were Ȝš or šȝ and *Mḥnty-n-ỉrty*. Others are now only known by their symbols, such as the Labrys or Double-axe, the

Mountains, the Sky-pole, and the Bull of the Sky. However, at least two lasted on in full vigour all through Pharaonic history. Their fates are curiously different. Seth, the storm-god, sank into the personification of all that was evil; Min developed Amûn, who was to become chief god of imperial Egypt.

A great deal that has come to light in this study indicates a similar antiquity for the rites. Such are, the preponderance of the deities of the prehistoric cities of Buto and Nekheb; the performance of the harvest festival with the primitive *bd·t*, emmer-wheat, although a better quality had long been grown in Egypt; the importance of Libya in the *sed*-festival and elsewhere.

Whatever else it may have been the *sed*-festival was one for inducing fertility in the fields. It was also extremely ancient, being held in Archaic days, and the importance of Libya in it suggests that it goes back to a time before the Nile Valley had been colonized. It was not a ceremony of the Osiris-religion as has so commonly been thought, but on the contrary the gods of the Old Religion are prominent everywhere in it.

The Pharaoh was emphatically divine. Indeed, Ramesses II's courtiers looked upon him as an ideal fertility-king, who was in himself the whole universe, and controlled it, thereby bringing his people prosperity and victory. The Pharaoh took part in the agricultural labours of the nation. In Archaic days he recorded the opening of the irrigation dykes, hoed the earth, and received a sheaf of *bd·t*. In the New Kingdom he ceremonially reaped a sheaf of the primitive *bd·t*, and, in later days again, it was to him that the prospects for the cattle and crops were revealed. All through history he performed the *sed*-festival, in one part of which he brought fertility to the fields. In the Nineteenth and

Twentieth Dynasties not only was there an insistence on the agricultural duties of the king, but also on his powers over the weather and the Nile. We know of this under Ramesses II, Merenptah, and Ramesses III inscriptionally, and in legend under Pherôs. This was the time of the recrudescence of Seth-worship. Besides joining in the agricultural activities of his people, in Pyramid times the divine Pharaoh was subject to a death which might be avoided. In this he emulated his great prototype, Seth the sky-god. Further, it is significant that ploughing the earth should be mentioned in this passage, and that for this the king should be likened to Shu the air-god. At a certain festival of hoeing the earth the sacrifice of Seth, and therefore presumably of the king who represented him, had been commuted in historic times for that of goats. The sacred animals of Typhon-Seth, we are told, were held responsible for the health of the people and the supply of water. Their duties were, therefore, the same as those of fertility-kings, who like them were incarnations of the storm-god. Human incarnations of Seth had various spans of life allotted to them, and among other marks they were known by their redness. One of these red people, the Pharaoh Nitocris, is said to have become a goddess and to have perished in the fire. This is what Plutarch says 'men of the colour of Typhon' used to do, and what those devotees of fertility, the adulteresses, did at the town called 'Red Soil'. Nitocris herself has become confused in story with a rosy-cheeked courtesan, Rhodopis. The ashes of some at least of these Seth-sacrifices were used as a rain-charm. In Egypt the king had generally been able to find a substitute since the Fourth Dynasty. But among the Libyans he was expected to undertake his destiny at least as late as the eighth century, and in Ethiopia until the third century B.C. One of the stories of Sabacon, however, implies that the

Libyo-Ethiopian kings had been tempted to follow Egypt's example and to rebel as early as the eighth century B.C. The Old Religion, and with it the sacrifice of the king, no doubt antedates the colonization of the Nile Valley. It was during the Second and Third Dynasties that a change began. It is observable in Zoser's move towards sun-worship, and hence away from the old gods. The breakaway came to a head under Khufu and Khafrê. After them the movement suffered a setback under Menkaurê and Shepseskaf, and even as late as the middle of the Fifth Dynasty Neuserrê, the builder of the splendid sun-temple, had to accept his seven lives from the gods of the Old Religion. By the Sixth Dynasty escape from the royal doom had become sufficiently common for Pepi to be able to say that he 'escapeth the day of death even as Seth escaped his day of death'. Did he propose to enact a death like the Mock King Abu Nerûz? In some way or another the Old Religion clearly kept a hold on the Pharaohs, for as late as the end of the Eighteenth Dynasty Akhenaton broke away once more. He was successful in keeping Amûn at bay for his lifetime, but his successor, Tutankhaton, had to return to his allegiance, and seems to have had to pay the final penalty of such kingships.

The classical folk-lore of Egypt is full of the death of Pharaohs, either by their own hands or by those of others. Nitocris, Sesoosis and Aegyptus are said to have committed suicide, a deed which in the cases of Cleopatra and evidently of Nitocris constituted an apotheosis. Busiris and Bocchoris were put to death; Bocchoris by his successor, just as the successor tried to do to Sesostris. The death was often by fire. The name Hercules which enters the Busiris story is that of a storm-god who was himself put to death by fire.

This folk-lore is also full of the escape of the Pharaoh by the sacrifice of a substitute. Such escapes were told of

Sesostris with every sign of a fertility-rite, of Anysis, and of Amasis. This we know to be a reflection of the facts, for by Pyramid times means had been found for both Seth and the king to escape their death. Later we also know that substitutes for Seth had been found in the form of goats. They were slaughtered, and their blood was ceremonially hoed into the ground. Undoubtedly men were also made to take the place of the king in the fire. Plutarch records it, and the last relic of the old sacrifice lingered on into the late nineteenth century in the person of the Mock King, Abu Nerûz, at the New Year carnival. The overthrow of enemies is at times represented at another fertility ceremony, the *sed*-festival, but there is no evidence as to whether they were substitutes for the king, or even sacrifices of any sort.

From the story of Ubaoner it is certain that in ancient Egypt adultery was expiated in the flames. Hence here again the spirit of fertility was freed from its human shrine by the age-old method. But such sacrifices, like those of the erring sacred animals of Seth recorded by Plutarch, were probably not official substitutes for the king but merely supernumerary. Herodotus' and Diodorus' story of the fertility-king Pherôs, the cultivator's wife, the adulteresses, and the 'sacred' or 'red' soil, is therefore substantially correct, as is Heliodorus' story of the fire-walking in Ethiopia. Such a ceremony as this latter certainly took place in the Eighteenth Dynasty, and may go back to Predynastic times, at which date a suitable trench full of ashes has been found.

The fertility theme runs through many of these classical stories. It occurs in the story of Pherôs, a cultivator, and adultery; in that of the taking of Sesostris' women by his would-be successor; in that of Cheops' prostitution of his own daughter, and in the confusion of Nitocris with a courtesan.

Blindness enters the legends of Anysis-Bocchoris, Sesoosis and Pherôs, and proves to be a common disability in practitioners of the sky-religion. In genuine Pharaonic religion it is found in Horus' loss of one or possibly of both eyes, and at the Thunderbolt-city of Letopolis, with its god 'He who is without eyes', and its shrewmouse that was sacred because it was thought to be blind.

Thus, the classical tales are not mere nonsense, but record details of the Old Religion and the horrors enacted under it. These may have impressed themselves upon the mind of the people, but again it may have been these that most nearly concerned the people, who probably still thought them to be desirable for the national welfare. The classical tales refer to the revolt of the Pharaohs from their doom in the Fourth Dynasty; to the recrudescence of Seth-worship in the Nineteenth Dynasty; finally to the resurgence of the old law in all its barbarity under Libyan influence in the eighth century B.C.

The doctrine of the control of the elements and all that it entailed dates from the times when the people were living in Libya, and were dependent upon the rain not upon the inundation of the Nile. When the change came in their methods of farming, the practice had to be adapted to the new conditions and the king had to undertake the control of the Nile. This is apparent under Tethmosy III, Ramesses II, Merenptah, and Ramesses III in history, and in legend under Pherôs and Aegyptus. The change is also to be seen in the performance of the old rainmaking sacrifices at the time of the rising of the Nile. It may be that the stories of the opening of the underground waters by the divine Nitocris and by Cheops relate to the same thing.

As in fertility-rites in many other lands, the numbers nine and seven are continually encountered. The sevenfold cycle seems to be the native one in Egypt, and the ninefold to have been imported from the north.

The prominence of Libya everywhere should be noted. The Imperishable Stars are connected with this land. They include the Great Bear, and the ancient Egyptian idea of this constellation as a bull's leg still survives in the western desert. In one form or another Libya enters largely into the *sed*-festival. In the scene of the presentation of the seven lives to Neuserrê the Nile-gods wear the Libyan penistasche, as does Zoser in one of the scenes of his *sed*-festival. The great harvest festival of the Nineteenth and Twentieth Dynasties was that of the old emmer-wheat of Libyan days. A number of the gods mentioned are either Libyan or can be traced to Libyan days. The sky-god *Ḥꜣ* and Seth's predecessor *Ꜣš* are not only ancient but Libyan, while Seth's sacred animals, the pig and the hippopotamus, go back to Libyan days. Seth's constellation was the Great Bear, and, as has just been shown, it had connexions with Libya. The redness so well known in the storm-god, Seth, was a characteristic of the Libyans. Later on, at any rate, Seth himself became important in Libya, as did the sky-god Amûn. Moreover, the name of this last may be connected with the Libyan word *amân*, 'water'. The sky-god Hercules was related to Amûn, and came to Egypt from Libya, when he sacrificed Busiris. His name was given to a definite king of the Libyan period, Osorkon. Heracleopolis, the city of Hercules, was a centre of Libyan power in the late New Kingdom, and one of the places where sacrifices were made for the fertility of the earth. The revival of the sacrifice of the king, whether of Busiris or Bocchoris, took place under the Libyans of the Twenty-Third and Twenty-Fourth Dynasties. Moreover, the 'Ethiopian' Sabacon, who sacrificed Bocchoris, was himself of Libyan extraction, and may have been subject to the same fate. Hence, there can hardly be any doubt that the sky-fertility-religion in Egypt was of Libyan origin, and the evidence suggests that it already existed in Libya in the earliest times.

All of the foregoing is completely outside the two well-known religions of Egypt, those of Rê and Osiris. It is in fact the Old Religion, of which Seth was one of the chief gods. An important factor in religious history in Egypt was clearly provided by continuous attempts by the Pharaohs to escape their fate under this Old Religion. This they did by encouraging sun-worship and making it the royal religion, as may be seen in the Old Kingdom and again under Akhenaton. Legend reflects this attitude in the story of Pherôs. But whatever may have been the attitude of the Pharaohs themselves, and perhaps of some of the educated classes, the Old Religion was too deeply rooted in the people to die out before such a newcomer as Rê or even Osiris. In fact, while these two long ago sank into the twilight of the gods, the Old Religion continued to hold the affections of the populace. Having survived the assault of Rê and the far more serious one of Osiris, the Old Religion, in the attenuated human sacrifice of the Abu Nerûz festival, survived those of Christianity and Islam for nearly nineteen hundred years.

APPENDIX

THE RISE OF RÊ- AND OSIRIS-WORSHIP

THERE is so much misapprehension as to Egyptian religion, especially in the non-Egyptological world, that a few words in addition may not be out of place. The general impression has been largely derived from the vague statements of syncretizing classical writers. They of course perpetuate so much as they were able to gather, and that unfortunately is only the religion as practised at the very end of Egyptian days. The impression is also gained from that form of Isis-worship which spread over the Graeco-Roman world during the first centuries of the Christian era. This was riddled with foreign philosophical and moralizing notions, and would no doubt have been quite unrecognizable by a native Egyptian, certainly by an Egyptian of an earlier age. To make the confusion worse there is to be found embedded in these writings a number of isolated statements which refer to an earlier period, and our authors often give them an explanation to make them fit with their own conceptions. Thus, to the non-Egyptologist Osiris and his fate at the hands of the 'wicked' Seth represents Egyptian religion. But actually this myth was a very slow growth, and it was not until quite late days that it had permeated nearly everything.

Similarly to the Egyptologist the Rê-religion added to Osiris-worship has outweighed everything else. This is due to the almost exclusive study of the texts, from the late ones backwards, where Rê has been intruded everywhere. The other gods are seen dimly as they appear through a haze of sun-worship. They are thus quite unintelligible. From the New Kingdom onwards nearly every god may wear the sun's disc or have Rê attached to his name, such as Amon-rê, Min-rê, Sebek-rê, Rê-harakhte, etc., etc. As a matter of fact many of these gods are sky-gods, whether representing the wind, air, rain, light, or the sky itself. It was, therefore, not difficult to approximate to them the most splendid emanation of the sky—the sun. It was easier still owing to the urge of the Pharaohs to seek refuge in Rê, and again owing to the existence of the great school of learning at Heliopolis, which was naturally not slow to take advantage of the opportunity. Hence, it comes about that so much of the religious literature that has come down to us has been written under sun auspices.

Actually such views as these are a misrepresentation of the state of affairs. Enough has been exposed in the fore-going pages, and in the articles therein quoted, to show that there was at least one vast, primitive, and ancient religion underlying the rest. No doubt there were others. In fact one may almost look upon Osiris- and Rê-worship as excrescences upon the fundamental religion of Egypt, which indeed they have hitherto obscured.

For us, who know that the sun is the source of light, it is difficult to realize that this is not self-evident to non-scientific man. Yet the really extraordinary thing is that the fact should have been discovered. Perhaps it came from analogy with the full moon, which is clearly a light-giver. The world becomes light at dawn long before sunrise, and it is almost full daylight before the sun comes up over the horizon. Equally it is still light when the sun is obscured by clouds. The primitive outlook that light is one thing and the sun another finds expression in the story of the Creation. In Genesis i, 3–5, it is said that God created the light and divided the light from the darkness, calling the one Day and the other Night. This was the first day. It was not until the fourth day that 'God said, Let there be lights in the firmament of the heaven', which were the stars and 'two great lights; the greater light to rule the day, and the lesser light to rule the night' (Gen. i, 14-19). Thus even as late as the writing of Genesis the sun, moon, and stars were only part and parcel of the sky, and light was still thought to exist without them. By this time, however, it had been appreciated that they were there 'to give light upon the earth'. The kind of outlook is perhaps exemplified in a discussion which the present writer had some years ago with a fellah of Upper Egypt. He said that Allah sent angels at night to bring back the sun from the west to the east. To the remark that someone must have seen that being done, the reply came: 'But how could they? It's dark!' Possibly subconsciously the sun was here not connected with the dissemination of light. In untutored thought the moon falls into a different category from the sun. Not only is it a definite light-giver, but by its phases becomes more noticeable. Besides, in warm climates, where one lives much out of doors, the world is a cheerier place on a bright moonlight night than on a dark moonless one. On the other hand, so long as it is day the sun is always there, and so attracts no attention. Thus, to primitive man the sun is quite an unimportant feature of the sky.

However, it has been postulated that Heliopolis held a leading position in Predynastic Egypt. Even if it did, this would not entail any importance for Rê at this time, nor is there any archaeological evidence that he was important. In fact the evidence points in the other direction; towards what is probable on general grounds. There must be some thousands of representations of sacred standards on the

Predynastic pottery. Of these Newberry has catalogued some hundreds,[1] and has shown the mountains to be extremely common and the thunderbolt not uncommon. These are symbols of the sky-gods, but no sun-symbol was found among those he collected. De Morgan, however, was more fortunate and he records a single instance of ⚲,[2] which is presumably the sun's disc on a pole. Thus, instead of being important in this age, the sun was so unimportant as scarcely to exist as an object of worship.

Like that of the Fourth Dynasty the age of the Second and Third Dynasties was one of religious unrest and struggle. The old sky-religion was divided against itself and by the end of the Second Dynasty Seth, the storm-god, had fought and lost his last battle with the already composite sky-god Horus. In the middle of this dynasty he had been victorious under the Seth-king Perabsen, but shortly afterwards he was conquered in the reign of the Horus-king Khasekhem, who became the Horus-and-Seth-king Khasekhemui (p. 65). It is now that the newcomer Rê, the sun-god, begins occasionally to appear upon the scene. Thus, early in the Second Dynasty king Neterymu refers to 'the City of Shem-Rê', recording its foundation as Schäfer reads it,[3] or its 'hacking up' (destruction) as Breasted takes it.[4] Neterymu's predecessor had been Nebrê, the first king to form his name on that of the sun-god, and between Perabsen and Khasekhemui came the second king to do so, Karê.[5]

---

[1] *Annals of Archaeology and Anthropology* (Liverpool), v, pp. 138–42.
[2] *Recherches sur les origines de l'Égypte*, 1897, p. 93, fig. 248, and Petrie, *Prehistoric Egypt*, Pl. xxiii, fig. 5, no. 16. Unfortunately the projections underneath the disc are not easy to understand. Are they rays?
[3] *Ein Bruchstück altägyptischer Annalen*, p. 24, no. 8 (published in *Abhandl. der K. Preuss. Ak. der Wiss.*, Berlin, 1902).   [4] *A.R.* i, § 125.
[5] Petrie, *History* (10th ed.), i, pp. 30, 34 and fig. 20.

The Second Dynasty thus provides the first two royal names of the type that later became usual. The process is continued in the Third Dynasty by Nebkarê,[1] and his successor Zoser took the title Rê-nub, 'The Sun of Gold'.[2] In the Fourth Dynasty the first true pyramid, a sun-symbol, had been built by Sneferu, and we have the names Dadfrê, Khafrê, and Menkaurê. Khafrê in the Fourth Dynasty and Sahurê in the Fifth may have used the title Sa-rê, 'Son of the Sun'.[3] Whether these inscriptions are contemporary or not,[4] one of Sahurê's immediate successors, Neuserrê, certainly used the title.[5] During the Fifth Dynasty we get kings calling themselves Sahurê, Neferirkarê, Neuserrê, Dadkarê. At the end of the dynasty we get our earliest copy of the Pyramid Texts, where Rê is thrust in everywhere; into texts which clearly come from the old sky-religion, and others which belong to Rê himself.

We do not even know where Rê came from. He certainly did not come from Heliopolis, which was not named after Rê, but was called Iunu, the On of the Bible, 'The Pillar-city'. There the sacred symbol was the pillar *iwn*, and Atum, whatever he may have been, was the original god, upon whom Rê was forced, making a compound deity called Rê-atum.[6] It was prophesied to Khufu of the Fourth

---

[1] Id. *op. cit.* I, p. 41.

[2] L. *D.* II, Pl. 2, f; Firth and Quibell, *The Step Pyramid*, Pls. 16, 39, 43.

[3] KHAFRÊ, Borchardt, *Statuen und Statuetten von Königen und Privat-leuten*, I, nos. 15, 17; SAHURÊ, Gauthier, *Le livre des rois*, I, p. 112.

[4] Borchardt considered these inscriptions to be later additions, *ZÄS*, 1898, p. 13. But then in *ZÄS*, 1892, p. 87, he also considered the blue tiles in the Step Pyramid to be additions of the Twenty-Sixth Dynasty. This idea has now been proved to be untenable. It was all part of a theory of wholesale restorations of the pyramids in Saitic times.

[5] Gardiner and Peet, *The Inscriptions of Sinai*, Pl. vi, 10.

[6] *Pyr.* §§ 145, 152, 154, 156, 158, 160. Cf. pp. 106, 107 *infra* for the Pillar.

Dynasty that the first three kings of the Fifth Dynasty should be divinely born of the wife of the priest of Rê of Sakhebu, and that the eldest of them should become high priest in Heliopolis.[1] Here is a definite statement, though not contemporary, that at that time Rê's city was not Iunu-Heliopolis, but an otherwise unknown place, Sakhebu. There is also a very broad hint that it was not until that period that he reached Heliopolis.

The origin of Rê is, therefore, obscure. While apparently he did exist in Predynastic days, he was then extremely unimportant. From the Second Dynasty onwards he began to creep into prominence, but it was not until the Old Kingdom that he began to acquire any importance. But from then onwards his advance was steady. His opportunity came through the patronage of the kings as an alternative to the saturnine Old Religion. It may well be that his worship was mainly a royal religion. Certainly the allegiance of the people was given to the Old Religion.

The development of Osiris was even later than that of Rê. We know nothing of him in Predynastic times. His headquarters, as known to us, were at _Ddw_, Busiris in the Delta, where, however, he was not the original god, but Anzety. Moreover, the sacred symbol there, the _dd_-pillar, after which the city was named, seems originally to have belonged to Seth.[2] We know nothing of Osiris until the late Fifth Dynasty, when he begins to appear in the funerary texts alongside of Anubis, an older god of the dead. In the Pyramid Texts Osiris is everywhere, yet some spells think

---

[1] The Westcar Papyrus, perhaps written in the Hyksos period, _c._ 1788–1580 B.C., Erman, _The Literature of the Ancient Egyptians_ (trans. Blackman), pp. 43, 45.

[2] Sethe, _Untersuchungen zur Geschichte und Altertumskunde Aegyptens_, x (_Dramatische Texte_), pp. 155, 156, no. 47 b.

of him as the enemy of the dead man.[1] It was not until the Sixth Dynasty that he reached Abydos, which was to become his holiest place of pilgrimage, and there he superseded the old Khenty-amentiu. He did not reach the position of national god of the dead until the Twelfth Dynasty. From then onwards his progress was one long triumph, culminating in all that we know from the Ptolemaic and Roman temple inscriptions and from the classical authors. Being a fertility-god who died and rose again he had much in common with the old Seth. Seth, as we know, personified the sky with its life-giving rain, a phenomenon which had ceased to have meaning in the rainless Nile Valley. Osiris personified fertility and the life-giving inundation of the Nile.[2] He was, therefore, more up-to-date than Seth, the storm-god, and was very real and necessary to the dwellers by the Nile. His religion may have been less crude and barbarous than that of Seth. If so, as elsewhere, the barbarities of the Old Religion would have gone to strengthen the view of the wickedness of the old god who withstood the progress of the new.

While the rising Osiris-religion had to try to suppress Seth with whom it came into competition, it was able to cope with Horus by adopting him as the son of Isis, wife of Osiris. This was still more unfortunate for Seth, for he had long ago been at enmity with Horus. The cause of his antagonism with Horus was, however, quite different from that with Osiris. With Osiris it was the outcome of competition between fertility-givers; the old rain-god out-of-date in the rainless Nile Valley, and the new up-to-date god of the waters of the Nile. Horus on the contrary was

---

[1] *Pyr.* §§ 145, 146, 350, 1267.

[2] Breasted, *Development of Religion and Thought in Ancient Egypt*, pp. 18–24.

7-2

no fertility-god or water-giver. He was a sky-god like Seth himself. But he was not a storm-god, but a god of light, as is shown by such forms as Harakhte 'Horus of the Horizon', etc. He was, thus, god of the bright sky like Apollo, with whom he was identified. Hence, as Seth was the storm-god, his quarrel with Horus was that of the storm with the calm, blue, bright sky. It was not the attack of the dark storm-clouds rolling up and obscuring the sun. Still less was it the perpetual struggle between daylight and darkness, i.e. between day and night. Hence, Seth never came into conflict with Rê, the sun-god. In fact he was taken into the boat of the sun, and there did yeoman service in repelling the great serpent Aapep.[1]

Instead of being the longed-for and blessed giver of life, Seth's rain had become the inconvenience that it still is in Egypt today.[2] Thus, the new conditions of life in the practically rainless Nile Valley were trebly unfortunate for Seth. In being out-of-date he became a nuisance to his people, and an offence to the two forces which did function for them beneficently; Horus the clear, cloudless sky, and Osiris the fertility of the Nile waters. Seth, thus, went the way of so many unsuccessful gods and became the personification of all evil—the very Devil himself.[3]

[1] Nagel, *Set dans la barque solaire* in *Bull. de l'instit. fr. d'arch. or.* (le Caire), xxviii, pp. 33–9.

[2] Already noted in the Twelfth Dynasty, when the man who is tired of life thinks of death as a variety of pleasant things. Among others he thinks of it 'as the ceasing of rain' and 'as clearing of the sky', Scharff, *Der Bericht über das Streitsgespräch eines Lebensmüden mit seiner Seele*, p. 56 and note 7 (published in *Sitzungsb. der Bay. Ak. der Wiss. Phil.-hist. Abt.*, 1937, Heft 9).

[3] If unsuccessful gods do not die out altogether, they either become sons, or assistants, or followers, of the new, or else they become devils as being adversaries of the new god who is good. Thus, Indra and Nasatya, who were gods in the fourteenth century B.C. and so survive in India today, have in Persia become arch-fiends of the newer

religion of Zoroaster (Hastings, *Encyclopaedia of Religion and Ethics*, s.v. *Demons and Spirits* (Persian), p. 620). Correspondingly in India the word *dēva* means 'god', while in Persia *daēva* means 'devil' (id. *op. cit.* p. 619). Christianity has everywhere called the old gods devils; S. Paul states categorically that the Gentiles 'sacrifice to devils' (I Cor. x, 20); the author of the book of Revelations (ii, 13) refers to the magnificent altar of Zeus at Pergamos as 'Satan's throne'; in the fourth century A.D. St Ephraim speaks of Heliopolis, where the cult of demons (*šēdhā*) was carried on, the demons of course being the heathen gods (*S. Patris Nostri Ephraem Syri Opera Omnia* (Rome, 1732–46) *Syriace et Latine*, II, p. 144. Commentary on Jeremiah xliii, 13); the mediaeval clerics spoke of the god incarnate of the Old Religion in Europe as 'the Devil' *tout simple*. Islam calls the Yezidis of Mesopotamia 'Devil-worshippers', and Tinia, the Etruscan Zeus, has now fallen in Tuscany to the status of an evil spirit or goblin of that name who spoils the crops in a great storm (Leland, *Etruscan Roman Remains in Popular Tradition*, p. 21).

ADDENDA

P. 31, n. 4. In the Twenty-Second Dynasty Seth's sexual (fertility) proclivities gave rise to this curse in the Dakhlah Oasis, 'Curse: The ass shall lie with him; the ass shall lie with his wife; his wife shall lie with his son', Spiegelberg in *Rec. de Trav.* xxv (1903), p. 195, l. 15, and p. 196.

P. 43. Yet other fair people are known from the monuments. In the Twelfth Dynasty foreigners are shown with yellowish skin, grey eyes, and red hair, beards, and whiskers, L. *D.* II, Pl. 141 = Newberry, *Beni Hasan* I, Pl. xvi; IV, Pl. xxiii, and p. 7. In the Eighteenth Dynasty some of the captives, who are making bricks, are of a pale colour, with paler reddish yellow hair. The eyes of one of them are blue, and of the others red, N. de G. Davies, *Paintings from the Tomb of Rekh-mi-rēᶜ at Thebes*, Pl. xvii. This supersedes L. *D.* III, Pl. 40, where the colours are much yellower and less accurate.

P. 48, n. 1. Who was ὁ τεταγμένος ἐπὶ τῶν ἱερῶν τῆς Αἰγύπτου, 'He who was appointed over the sacrifices of Egypt', or as it is often read, 'He who was appointed over the priests of Egypt' by emending ἱερῶν to ἱερέων? If he had merely intended to write 'the high-priest' why should Josephus have invented so curious a circumlocution instead of using the simple ἀρχιερεύς? Actually, of course, there was no high-priest of all Egypt, but very many local ones up and down the country. If 'He who was appointed over the sacrifices of Egypt' really represents an actual functionary, he would be one whose duties had to be explained to the foreign reader for whom Josephus was writing.

As a matter of fact I think such a person can be found.

Akhenaton, as we know, fled from Amûn and persecuted him, deleting his name and figure from the sculptures. It seems significant, therefore, that there was one priest who shared with Amûn in the heretic king's hatred. He was the *sem*-priest, whose figure Mr N. de G. Davies once told me has been specially hacked out of the paintings. In the Opening of the Mouth ceremonies he was connected with sacrifice to the extent of superintending the slaughter of the bull, and himself offering the leg and the gazelles and the goose.[1] All of these of course were Sethian in nature. The *sem*-priesthood was very ancient and the holder of that office played a very important part in the *sed*-festival. He was in the closest attendance upon the king throughout the ceremonies. In particular, he installed him upon the throne,[2] invested him with the *was*- and crook-sceptres,[3] and presented him with the bow and arrows.[4] In fact so closely is the *sem*-priest connected with the king that von Bissing and Kees speak of him as the 'Königspriester'. In the New Kingdom the *sem*-priest develops into the *sem-inmutf* or merely the *inmutf*-priest, and numerous examples show that the crown prince filled this role. In fact the unique position of the *sem* (*inmutf*) rests upon his identity with the successor to the throne. Later the *sem* is often, like the high-priest of Memphis, an office which in older as in later times was mostly filled by a royal prince.[5] In the New Kingdom the *sem* is well known as an important

[1] Budge, *The Book of Opening the Mouth*, I, pp. 163, 164, 182; II, pp. 19, 20, 35, 36, 98, and cf. pp. 132, 172.

[2] Bissing and Kees, *Re-Heiligtum*, II, Pl. 16, no. 39; cf. Id., *Untersuchungen zu den Reliefs aus dem Re-Heiligtum des Rathures*, I, p. 98 (published in *Abhandl. Bay. Ak. der Wiss., Philos.-philol.-hist. Klasse*, XXXII (1922)).

[3] *Re-Heiligtum*, II, Pls. 16, 17, nos. 39, 42.

[4] *Op. cit.*, Pls. 18, 19, nos. 44 *b*, *c*, 45 *b*.

[5] *Untersuchungen*, I, p. 67.

priest of Ptah of Memphis, and two high-priests of Amûn are known to have added this priesthood to their other dignities.[1] Ramesses II's son, Khaemwas who was adopted as heir, was both *sem* and high-priest of Memphis,[2] and in Ptolemaic times *sem* is given at least once as a subordinate title of the high-priest of Memphis.[3]

At Memphis there was also a priest with a very curious insignia, and he was sometimes the high-priest.[4] He wore a collar representing an anthropomorphized jackal, or possibly two jackals. While we were in the press Dr

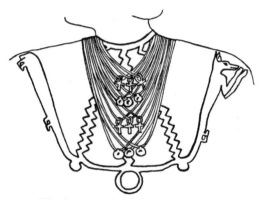

Kha-bau-seker's collar and necklace.

Margaret Murray's book, *Saqqara Mastabas*, II, appeared, and in it she studies this priesthood on pp. 1–6. On one occasion the wearer of the jackal collar also wears a necklace from which hang six ankhs (signs of life) and six balls or discs. This was Kha-bau-seker of the Third Dynasty,

[1] M. Stolk, *Ptah*, pp. 35, 38, 39.
[2] Petrie, *History* (10th ed.), III, pp. 84, 85; Brugsch, *Thesaurus*, p. 957.
[3] Brugsch, *Dictionnaire géographique*, p. 1368.
[4] Erman in *ZÄS*, 1895, pp. 22, 23; e.g. Ranefer in the Fifth Dynasty, and Khaemwas in the Nineteenth.

and he was not the high-priest. His priesthoods are significant. He had much to do with Anubis, for besides wearing the jackal collar he held two priesthoods of his.[1] He also had much to do with Seth, for he not only held a priesthood of his, but was even priest of the divine emblem of the Oxyrhynchite nome which was one of Seth's headquarters.[2] There was only one other deity, Seshat, of whom he was priest, but she seems to be without significance here. Thus, Kha-bau-seker was almost entirely concerned with Seth the rain- and fertility-god who was sacrificed, with Anubis the death-god, and with six lives or periods of life. Dr Murray very naturally compares all this with the story that Mycerinus was given six years to live and should die in the seventh (Hdt. II, 133), and also with the fact that Anubis gave seven ankhs to Neuserrê under the supervision of Wazet-Buto from whom Mycerinus had received his message (p. 47). She also notices that Kha-bau-seker's name is compounded with that of the god of the dead in Memphis. It means 'The glory of Seker shines'. Hence, it looks as if there were some priest in Egypt whose duty it was to announce his span of life to the Pharaoh. It also looks as if he were in some way connected with Memphis, and that he was liable to be the successor to the throne. It has already been seen (pp. 5, 29, 49) that in many lands the reigning king has to be sacrificed by his successor. Further, it will be remembered that while in the story it was 'He who was set over the sacrifices of Egypt' who sent to Sesostris, it was his would-be successor who attempted to put him to death. The crown-prince would be the natural successor and he was, or was represented by, the *sem*-priest, whom Akhenaton hated along with Amûn of

[1] Murray and Sethe, *Saqqara Mastabas*, II, pp. 4, 11, nos. 10, 11.
[2] Id. *op. cit.* pp. 4, 11, nos. 12, 14.

the sky- and fertility-religion. Did Akhenaton hate the *sem*-priest because in the normal course of events he would have been the channel through whom the dread summons would have come? Again, was it not some later *sem*-priest, or some later wearer of Kha-bau-seker's collar and necklace, whose duties Josephus records in his phrase 'He who was appointed over the sacrifices of Egypt'?

P. 79. A curious coincidence may suggest that the separation of Egypt and the North into areas of seven and nine may go back to very ancient times. The round dance is a well-known ceremony of the old fertility-religion. At Cogul in eastern Spain it is performed by nine women (Murray, *The God of the Witches*, Pl. ix, facing p. 102), while it is performed by seven women in a rock-engraving from Egypt (H. A. Winkler, *Völker und Völkerbewegungen im vorgeschichtlichen Oberägypten im Lichte neuer Felsbilderfunde* (Stuttgart, 1937), pp. 11, 12, 22, and fig. 26, where only six of them could be got into the photograph). The Cogul paintings are Late Palaeolithic in date, while the Egyptian engraving probably belongs to the Feather-dress people. These people seem to have entered Upper Egypt by way of the Red Sea during the First Predynastic Age.

P. 97. The accompanying figure represents the *iwn*-pillar after which the city of Iunu (Heliopolis) was named. It is taken from a sculpture showing Ramesses II standing before Atum, and setting up 'the *iwn*-pillar of the Bull of Iunu for Atum'.[1] The pillar has nothing to do with Rê, but belongs to his predecessor Atum, or, more accurately still, to the sacred bull of the city, Mnevis. In fact it is identified with him, having his head set upon it here as else-

---

[1] L. D. III, Pl. 147, b. The scene stands next to one of Min's *shnt*-pole with the climbing Nubians, Porter and Moss. *Topographical Bibliography*, II, p. 47, South Side, nos. 3, 4.

where.[1] It, then, is one more of these bull pillars of which Egypt had so many. There was Min's *šḥnt*-pole and his bull, the pillar of Nubia and the Bull of the Sky, the pillar of eye-paint and the Bull of the Sky, the pillar of the Aphroditopolite nome and the Great Bull, and at Cusae the sky-pole *wḥ* was personified by a bull.[2] In the light of all this the *iwn*-pillar and Mnevis were no doubt sky-symbols like the others. If so, Heliopolis would originally have been yet another city devoted to sky-worship. This belonged to a time long before Rê settled there, and imposed himself to such an extent that the Greeks thought of the city as peculiarly his, and called it after him Heliopolis, the City of the Sun.

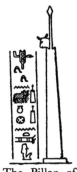

The Pillar of the Bull of Heliopolis.

[1] E.g. Möller in *ZÄS*, xxxix, p. 72, fig. i; Naville, *The Festival Hall of Osorkon*, ii, Pl. ix, fig. 9.

[2] *JEA*, xxi, pp. 163, 164, 168, and *OLZ*, 1932, cols. 521 ff.

INDEX

[113]

CAMBRIDGE: PRINTED BY W. LEWIS, M.A., AT THE UNIVERSITY PRESS